Emmanuel's
Book III

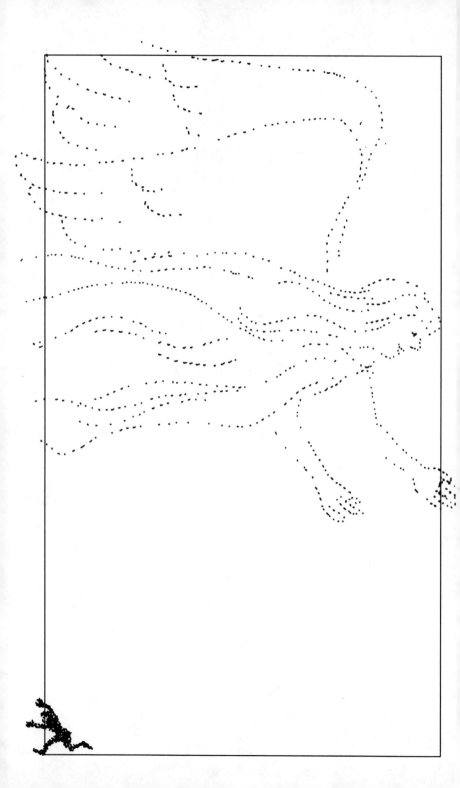

Emmanuel's
Book III

What Is an Angel Doing Here?

Compiled by
Pat Rodegast and
Judith Stanton

Illustrated by
Roland Rodegast

Bantam Books

New York   Toronto   London   Sydney   Auckland

EMMANUEL'S BOOK III
A Bantam Book / November 1994

Library of Congress Cataloging-in-Publication Data

Emmanuel (Spirit)
    What is an angel doing here? / compiled by Pat Rodegast and Judith
Stanton.
        p. cm.—(Emmanuel's book: 3)
    ISBN 0-553-37412-5 (pbk.)
    1. Spirit writings.   2. Emmanuel (Spirit)   I. Rodegast, Pat.
II. Stanton, Judith.   III. Title. IV. Series: Emmanuel (Spirit).
Emmanuel's book: 3.
BF1301.E526   1994
133.9'3—dc20   94-16006
                                                                      CIP

Published simultaneously in the United States and Canada

Bantam Books are published by Bantam Books, a division of Bantam
Doubleday Dell Publishing Group, Inc. Its trademark, consisting of the words,
"Bantam Books" and the portrayal of a rooster, is Registered in U.S. Patent and
Trademark Office and in other countries. Marca Registrada. Bantam Books,
1540 Broadway, New York, New York 10036.

PRINTED IN THE UNITED STATES OF AMERICA

BVG   0 9 8 7 6 5 4 3 2

Contents

Introduction

The question you all live with is "Who am I?
Who am I really,
behind the masks of my human self?
Who am I beyond my historic definitions?"

There is a moment
when memory begins to awaken.

"Memory of what?" you ask.

Memory of your true nature...
your angelhood.

You have all been taught
to be much too frightened and too well behaved
to ever announce such a discovery.
So you have kept it secreted
away inside the sanctuaries of your hearts,
this wondrous *Self*, this real *You*...

As you have walked your lives,
there have been moments of need,
despair, pain, terror when you have cried out
to know a greater truth.
The human heart burst forth from its bondage
and called to the heavens in the name of Love.

So we meet in the name of that call—
in the name of that Love.
What was the call asking?
It was asking for truth.

The teachings in this book are offered
to ease the way from forgetting
back into the light of your remembered Divinity,
your angelhood.
I want to promise you that there is a way.
It is one in its purpose
and individual in its manner.
You will all come to the ultimate wisdom
of your true *Selves*. It is inevitable.
That is the purpose of your journey.

The heart is the doorway to wisdom.
You *are* your love.
Waste not one more moment
in your obedience to fear.
Fear was the vehicle for entering the illusion.
Love is the way Home.

So let us begin.
With your permission, allow me to escort you
through the pages of this book.
The purpose? Truth. The result? Freedom.
The teacher? Your own dear *Selves*.
For there is nothing you do not already know
in that secret, holy place within you
where the Angel dwells.

Some things to remember:

You do not have to prepare for life.

You do not have to avoid life.

You do not have to monitor life.

You do not have to solve life.

You do not have to protect life.

You do not have to fear life.

The issues of life are of no importance.

*The essence of all things
must be sought with a loving heart.*

What seems to be is not.

What you seek outside, you already own.

*The gathering of all experience
is only to know the nature
of the Love therein.*

*Enjoy the journey.
Your return tickets Home
are guaranteed.*

Emmanuel

Emmanuel's
Book III

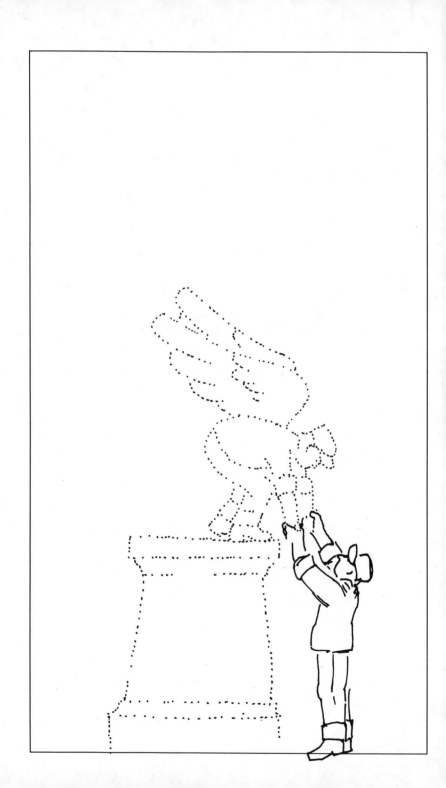

1
The Angel on the Rock

Be comfortable with your humanness.
But don't believe in it.

Take a giant step in faith.
I want you to believe in Angels.

You are not the limited human beings
that you think you are.
You are Divine energy
which has access to many universes.
At this moment in time,
you simply have chosen
a learning experience
on this particular planet.
Yet, you are greater
than the finite experiences
of this Earth.
In order to know yourselves,
and perceive the subtler levels of things,
you need to realize
what great Beings *You* are.

Each of your family members and friends
has also chosen to be human, and is greater
than you perceive him or her to be.
Remember, though the body was formed
by human beings, your souls have been created
by eternal and perfect Love.
When you tune into the energy of the Creator,
the finite portions of you
suddenly become free to manifest greatness
in this lifetime.
That will affect all other lifetimes,
past and future.
Since your concept of linear time
is only a concept and not a reality at all,
what you do *now* has its effect on all "time."

*Right NOW
is such a time of possibility.*

I do not mean to trivialize the humanness
that you have all worked so hard to sculpt
into some workable self-presentation,
but you are only part human.
The other part of you is Angel.
All things are in a state of pulsation
on your planet.
All things have a negative
and a positive aspect.
All things are flickering
in and out of form. So are you.

When you pulsate into your humanness,
your attention is aligned with that aspect.
It seems as if you are always human.
When you connect with the Angel side
of the pulsation,
you recognize that you are always spirit as well.
You blink in and out of the world of illusion
with the regularity of a ticking metronome.

**Can you give us an example
of how this pulsation works?**

When you are in spirit,
you are creating the next moment
of human consciousness.
When you are in human consciousness,
you are breathing out the world
to which you will return
after you have vanished
for a time fragment so minuscule
that your languages have
no words for it.

With every breath you take,
you enter into a new creation.
You are not struggling to stay alive
in some continuum that marches on without you.
Each one of you breathes the creative force
that brings to life, moment by moment,
the human world and all that is upon it.
In the pulsation you move from remembering
who *You* are into forgetting
and back to remembering again.

If, at one instant,
every conscious living soul upon the planet
agreed to stop breathing,
not only would that be the end of the breathers,
it would dissolve as well
everything that was ever manifested.
Mind might conclude,
"So the people would die
but the plants would still be alive."
I tell you that they would not.
Nothing upon the planet would continue
if every Angel upon it refused to breathe
the next breath of creation.

"Why, then," you ask,
"if we are continuing
to create with every breath,
are we doing such a messy, cruel job of it?"

It is entirely up to you
how it is you choose to build the next moment.
If you choose Love,
then the next moment is created
in the name of that Love
and all things on the planet
are changed by that breath.
If you breathe with fear,
then you squeeze the next moment
of your human life into the narrow bonds
of that illusion.

Do not perceive in this
some false sense of responsibility.
Life requires only your willingness
to be who *You* are.
Nothing is the same from one breath to the next,
not you, nor planet Earth beneath your feet.

If you could view with a fresh lens
what transpires as you breathe one simple breath,
you would be astounded.
When we in spirit urge you to
"breathe into the next moment
and choose Love,"
that is not just some casual game.
Each breath is a miracle.

During your days,
let your breathing remind you
that you are also an Angel.
Each time you become aware of your angelhood,
with just that one second of realization,
critical mass has shifted in favor of spirit.
If you remain connected to the greater *You*
for even three breaths,
you live more in truth than you do in illusion.

Have I confused you?
I hope so,
for in trying to figure out
at which time it is *not* there,
mind will be kept so busy that the heart
can be allowed more room
in the center of your life.

Can we notice this pulsation, Emmanuel?

The pulsation can be observed in its entirety
only when one is willing to lift a bit
beyond the pulsation itself.
As long as you are focused in your humanness,
it is difficult to perceive the shift,
since you see only half a movement.

The pulsation is extremely rapid, of course,
or you would notice your own absence.
As you grow up, it becomes so habitual
that you cease to notice what is taking place,
but the small child remembers.

Do you recall, in first or second grade,
those wondrous moments
when you looked out of the classroom window
and "disappeared"?
You were no longer the child sitting at the desk.
You had become everything and anything.
You blew with the wind.
You touched the sun.
You grew as a flower. You were light.
You lived your fantasy.
In those moments, you were close
to contacting your Angel side.

Has it occurred to you now
that in times of longing to escape,
it is not an unknown you reach for
but a solid memory?
In meditation or when you fall asleep,
do you not sometimes experience
the rush of wind, the feeling of freedom,
a sense of abandon?
Often when one is aware of Divine presence,
it is because one touches one's Angel half.

These things are available to you
not only when your mind is silenced.
They are present all the time.
It is your intellect that delays the experience
by its granted position of authority
in your lives.

Is there a similar pulsation
where you are, Emmanuel?
Do you blink on and off?

The pulsation is only into illusion and out of it.
We rest in a much more benign climate.

As you blink toward us we reach.
As you blink away we bless.

Can we reach out of our illusion?

Your bodies are ninety-nine percent space
wherein the Angel abides.
You limit yourselves to the identities
you were given as the necessary gear
for your safety.
You have walked masked and costumed,
probing here and there,
letting out a seam, undoing a button,
but always honoring to a great
extent the original outfit.

When angelhood awakens,
all the seams are burst.
The child, schooled in fearful modesty,
wonders, "What am I going to do now?"

You are going to free yourselves
from the distress of limitation.
Here is a practice to help you
expand your self-image.

Close your eyes
and bring your attention inside the body.
Rather than perceiving the body
as the familiar "you," solid matter,
allow yourselves to imagine that
You, the Angel,
are literally wearing a physical form.

Feel or see the molecular structure
of your bodies not as solid,
but as spacious,
with just enough physicality
to dust the spirit.
You are not the density
that you thought you were.
You are more Grace than molecule.

Let yourselves perceive the pores of your
skin as openings through which the Light
can shine in and out.

Allow yourselves to expand
through the openings into the outer world
until you come to an unthought, organic stop.

When you come to this place of rest, you
have touched who You really are.

It may feel as though you, as Angel,

have no boundaries.
Indeed, you do not! You are God.
You are All-That-Is.
When you can allow that vastness, you begin to see
how an Angel can exist
within the human form.

You, as perfect Love,
chose to enter into a very tiny body.
You cannot hope that such a body
can represent with fidelity
the truth of the greatness that just entered it.
Nor can you expect the human illusion
to understand the greatness of its Creator.
But there is no requirement
that an Angel compress itself
entirely into solid matter.
Wisdom can live anywhere.
In any circumstance,
there is room for the Angel.

You are an Angel first.
You are a human being second.

How do you think Love flows
from a physical body?
If it were tightly sealed, Love could not escape,
and yet you hear Love's call across continents,
although your physical ears
may not register it as such.

Since *You* are not solid matter,
the world of physical material
does not have to be seen as so solid,
so controlling, so impenetrable, so unyielding.
Knowing there is a little more room
for yourself in your world,
you will find it more manageable.
You will ultimately discover
that the world is meant to be a place
of spacious adventure,
not only of pain and suffering.

Acknowledging your angelhood
does not mean that you despise
your human condition.
Spirit loves its physicality
or it would not have chosen to become human.
It is time to blend both parts of you.

You the Angel
belong with you the human being
in every moment of your life.
When you feel hopeless, depleted,
lonely, or frightened,
that is because spirit,
your essence of perfect Love,
has not been allowed to walk
with you the human being.
As one grows accustomed
to wearing the lenses of human fear,
the truth becomes not only less and less available,
but less and less sought after,
until some time of enormous darkness
or enormous light,
when one's entire belief system
experiences a transformation.

Each of you holds,
secluded within you somewhere,
that holy moment
when the time-clock
of the soul's journey says,
"Now it is time to reverse direction
and head for Home."

During each lifetime
you come through carefully planned
and executed life experiences—
planned by the soul,
not consciously by the human being.
You bring with you your own teachers:
fears and beliefs
you may have carried for centuries,
in order to create your physical workshop
to honor the gift of Light
You were called to bring.
All things direct you to understand
that there is a greater *Self*
that cannot be aligned
with the limiting definition of self
that you have accepted.
All that transpires is designed by *You*, Angel,
to walk the adventure of humanness,
ultimately remembering who *You* are.

With that perspective clearly held,
there is not one moment of your life
that does not offer you the opportunity for unity.
So regard your humanness
as a great act of Spirit.
You need not struggle in duality to become One.
As you choose Love,
you naturally allow that unity.
Thus your reality transforms.

I am Angel and I am human.
I am One.

To remember who you are may take a lifetime.
Sometimes it takes only a second.
Your life is filled, day by day,
with moments of remembering.
You disregard them as imagination
or foolishness.
Every day that *You* are present in your life,
the Angel is present.
Take heart. You are so much more
than the fearful costume you wear.
You are so much greater
than the masks behind which
you hide your faces of innocence.
You are not only the children of God,
but God Itself.
Do not be discouraged.
You will remember.
The Angel was called into the human fray
to light the way.

How do we know when we touch the Angel?

When you experience joy, excitement,
passion and humor, you know
that you are walking with your Angel.
The human mind imagines
that Angels must be the soul of decorum,
altogether serious, willing to walk in a world
that is blind to them,
continually doing good works.

Let me introduce you to another sort of Angel:
the Angel of vivacity, the Angel of humor,
the Angel of enthusiasm, the Angel of curiosity.
If you were not Angels such as these,
would you have become intrigued
with human form again and again?

The mind's confusion is not the heart's wisdom.
Ask yourself now, "Which do I choose
to be my guide, my mind or my heart?"
Fear or Love?
The answer is simple. Love.
Swiftly mind steps in
before you have completed your response
and says, with seeming good will,
"But tell me...how do I do it?"

Tell your mind with compassion,
"Mind, the business of the heart
is not your business.
You are here to deal with a linear world,
to learn the vocabulary of verbal exchange.
As to angelhood,
you simply do not have the organic capacity
to understand."

Your strength will come
from standing in the center
of a place no one can see,
knowing what no one can verify,
and dancing to a tune
no one else can hear.

**Where are you, Emmanuel,
when you are not speaking through Pat?**

I am everywhere Love is and so are *You*.

**I have been accustomed to thinking of the inner mystery of
myself as God or Divine. You use the word "Angel." Is it all
the same?**

Absolutely, as long as you allow God
to be who *You* are.
The concept of God has, traditionally,
been given such awesome, distant, historic vastness.
Angels are more manageable.

What is the state we know as enlightenment?

Such a state involves the perception
of two realities at once.

When one moves to the awareness
where all things are seen as perfect
and therefore as dancing light
while one is still holding profound respect
for the human experience,
one becomes a bridge to both worlds.
That, I would say,
is enlightenment in physical form.

When physical form is done with,
then one can erase "enlightenment"
and simply pencil in "Homecoming."

Is it possible to live enlightened in the world?

Yes, but you will not then see the world
as you do now. Your lenses will clear
and you will see nothing but Angels
walking in the masquerade
of their own adventure.

When I say you are Angels,
that is exactly what I mean.
I am not using a metaphor.
I am not just choosing a pleasant word.
I am stating what I know to be true.
You are Beings of Light.

Let me urge you again to be who *You* are.
You will then fulfill every dream
you have ever had,
merely by that one simple commitment
to trust yourselves.
When your human hearts
are in accord with the Angel's mission,
you experience bliss, absolute delight,
and joy, for no reason that will satisfy the mind.
You find yourselves daring to reach
beyond the stars.

Don't let your human costumes fool you.
Don't allow your belief to be suppressed
by the intellect's demand for proof.
Until you believe something,
there is nothing to be proven.
It is your belief
that has brought this entire planet into reality.
It is your belief
that has brought you again and again
into human form,
and it is your belief
that fills All-That-Is
with the Light of your perfect Love.

As long as you are Angels,
you are involved
in the Divine creation of all things.
As long as you are human,
you will have great trouble accepting that.
Don't wait for proof.
Believe...and then allow the truth to manifest.

Now, of what benefit can all this information be?

Let it be a comfort
to those who believe
that they must always
be the solid rock
and not the Angel standing on it.

2
What Is an Angel Doing Here?

Love comes to find Itself,
and then calls forth bodies to wear.

If we were Angels in the Oneness,
why would we choose to leave it
to come to a place like planet Earth?

Remember you are gods,
and as such you are curious and adventuresome.
When *You* are in Oneness,
You touch that Love constantly
with gratitude, joy, and bliss,
but then you wondered,
as is your unique nature,
how it might be possible to know Love
outside that eternal perfection.
This creative curiosity brought you
into the journey of human adventure.

Is there any other way to go beyond Love
except into the fabricated mirage that Love is not,
that perfection is not,
that God is not,
in fact, that *You*, in the essence of your being,
are not?
So you created this small pocket of illusion
where love seems not to be,
and you entered it, Angels all, to explore.

There is no journey more holy.
There is nothing more courageous
than your willingness to be present
in this world in the name of Love Itself.
There is no one wiser than *You*, in your Divinity,
wrapped within the embrace
of your humanness.

"Strange journey," your minds are saying.
"Didn't we take a big risk in leaving?"

Angels do not believe in risk.
You wanted to worship All-That-Is,
to serve Love however It can be served.
Is that not a noble purpose?

You are humorous Angels.
An Angel removed,
who walks with careful, pious tread,
would not begin to consider
donning the rough-and-tumble suit
of humanity.

You who have walked a human life
and have come to a moment of realization
of the perfection of Love within yourselves
know what an enlightening experience it is,
as though an entirely new universe
has opened up. It is the remembering of Home.

You have all labored to create
a plane of consciousness that has chosen
to leave the Oneness—not in rebellion,
not in punishment,
but in worship.
You are called by the Love
that exists within that illusion
to bring the Light of your truth
into the forgetting self.
The moment of birth
is the giving of that gift.

You *are the creator
creating with every breath.*
You *are the wellspring
of All-That-Is.*

Mind asks, "If we can create anything,
why couldn't we come up
with something better than this?"

Although this may not have been
your most explainable creation,
your purpose is a worthy one.
You are all here,
not only for that existential purpose,
but because now you are woven
into the fabric of your human world.
You have been here so many times.
You have worshiped. You have suffered.
You have died. You have laughed.
You have given birth. You have mourned.
You have a deep familiarity
with those with whom you walk.
When they cry out for Love,
can you turn away?

In order to bring Light into the darkness,
you too must enter into that darkness.
One does not come to the doorway
of an obscure cave and illuminate it
merely by standing outside.
One enters the depths and, in that moment
of courage and supreme Love,
transforms the darkness
forever back into Light.

You shine your absolute presence
wherever forgetting casts its pall—
a simple task
yet vast and magical.

It all seems so difficult.

Your human life is a journey.
It is not a prison sentence.
It does not imply
that you did something wrong in Heaven
and were told to go out and learn a few things
before you returned repentant.
Your life is your gift to the planet.
Love called and perfect Love always responds.
You said yes.

Even in your humanness,
shielded from awareness of your angelhood
by the mask of your mortal personality,
You are still that Divine and perfect Love
that *You* have always been
and will always be.

When *You* leave the Oneness,
You forge a bridge connecting you
to the family of your choice.
You accept all the family "givens"
and hold them almost sacred.
You grow so accustomed to them
that you fail even to offer challenge.
Why, you almost believe you were
born with those chains around your wrists
and ankles.

As the Angel,
there is nothing beyond *Your* reach,
but when you are human and very young,
that bridge between you and family
becomes a necessary lifeline to your existence.

Then comes a time
when the noble longing of the heart
begins to flower,
when the wisdom of who *You* truly are
begins to emerge.
You recall your dream and thereby give it form.
This challenges every fiber
of that familial makeshift span.
Thus you are freed to become a conscious part
of the lighted bridge
between human and spirit.

**Is there anything that I, as an Angel, can do about
the massive suffering I see around me every day?**

A great deal.
The first thing an Angel can do,
having remembered who he or she is,
is to address the circumstances
of human experience without
holding the hand of fear.
Have you any idea how frightened you are
most of your lives?
You bury it so well
that most of you do not even perceive it
as fear anymore.
It has become habitual behavior.

Do you remember
how it was before you knew that you
were supposed to be afraid?
Afraid of what?
Anything. Everything.
Afraid to fall, afraid to lose,
afraid to die, afraid to care,
afraid to believe.

You have to live your way through your lives.
You cannot simply think them.
If you are to hesitate
at the door of mind's approval,
you will remain sitting in despair.
If you are willing to walk forth
where your heart calls,
you will find yourselves, moment by moment,
changing the consciousness of your world.
This is not an exaggeration.
This is who *You* are.

Your heart breaks because someone is in pain.
Your caring is the voice of God,
whether it is spoken audibly
or given tangibly or felt within your heart.
Therein lies all the power in the universe.

The doubting mind
would say, "Just give me a little sign
that my caring has helped.
Let me get a letter from Cambodia or Africa
that tells me someone
felt the touch of my hand."

There are many who,
if they knew to whom to address such a missive,
would send it.
They do not have the words
or the postal facility
to tell you that they felt a moment of Grace
and wondered from whence it came.
Perhaps they turned
to thank a stranger on the street.
Perhaps they prayed with gratitude
to an unseen God.
It doesn't matter how it manifested.
Your love has touched them.

Why is life so complicated?
People have so many worries.
My brother was laid off
and his entire life seems to be unraveling.

What is an Angel doing on the bread line?
The Angel is tasting the flavors of fear.
When a human being becomes aware
that he has come to do exactly that,
he will begin to recognize
that not only does fear stand in the bread line,
but a whole group of Angels
are standing there as well.

When that particular Angel
comes to such a realization,
he will begin to look around and see
with new eyes those who were labeled
by the mind as destitute, ne'er-do-well,
disadvantaged, or endangered.
He will see them all
as courageous Beings of Light
who have chosen to come together
at that moment and stand in the illusory line
in the name of illusory want.
The moment such a realization dawns,
that Angel has become wealthy.

There is no danger.
How could there be an endangered Angel?
Are there people who are trembling
at what they perceive is the ruin
of their lives?
Many.
They have come to a point
where they must question the meaning of *Self*.
Who am I?
Who are these people?
What illusion brought us together?
What is to be learned here?
What is the truth of this?

There is nothing more enlightening to do
than to look for the truth
in life's daily happenings.
Pay heed now,
for life will swiftly change.

Nothing remains
more than a moment.
Then, since the nature of creation
is to create,
another unique moment appears.

Here are some questions for your introspection.

Consult the wisdom
that rests beneath your mind's tyranny.
If, right now, you were absolutely sure
that you really are an Angel,
that you are eternal,
that you come from perfect Love
and will return to perfect Love,
what would you do with your life?

Are there any particular goals
you would pursue without the need
to be reasonable?

From which demands
would you release yourself?

What "history" would you forgive?

What judgments, dear one,
would you stop directing at yourself
and your world?

What is keeping you
from living your life as an Angel
right now?

You once said, Emmanuel,
that there are nights when we go forth
from our dreams and become Angels to others.
Could you tell us more about this?

Having accepted as a possibility
that you are not just your human body,
then it becomes reasonable
that when your body goes to sleep
and the intellect blessedly quiets down,
there is no need for you to remain
within the physical form.
Bodies adhere to the pull of gravity.
Love does not,
and Angels do not require sleep.

Sometimes your angelhood lifts in sleep,
traveling around the planet
to answer the call of Love.
You become visible,
indeed recognizable at times,
as a firmly embodied human being
in some other part of the world.
If your heart aches
at the picture of a starving child,
then that night there is a very good chance
that you will go and be the peace,
the comfort, perhaps even the vehicle Home
for that child.
Do not let sleep disguise the truth
of who *You* are.

Your Light reminds others
of their Light.

**Is there any way we can remember
these trips out of the body?**

*To remember where you have gone
and what you have done, as you awaken
and before you are fully in your body,
let yourself write upon a piece of paper
or speak softly into a recording device
what it is you* hope
you did the past night.

*I use the word "hope" deliberately.
It is a soft word.
It opens the heart and goes beyond the mind.
If you can listen to what you* hope
*you accomplished the night before,
in a very short time
the memory will come.*

There are no words
in the languages of your countries
to honor the wondrous gift that you bring.
You are not aliens to this planet,
though it is not your home.
You are the creators of it
and *You* are the Light of it.
Notice I did not say you are rescuers.
No one needs rescue,
but everybody requires Love.

**How do we know when we are doing our work
on the planet?**

The forces of Light are gathering
in those who have come to hear and to see
and to remember. Throughout your day,
ask yourselves, "What would an Angel do now?"
When you awaken in the morning ask,
"Why is an Angel here?"
If there were no purpose for your presence,
You, the Angel
would have remained at Home.

Remember that where *You* are,
perfect Love is.
Do not seek for linear definition.
Simply ask, "What is an Angel doing here?"
If you align that question with Love,
you will hear exquisite responses.

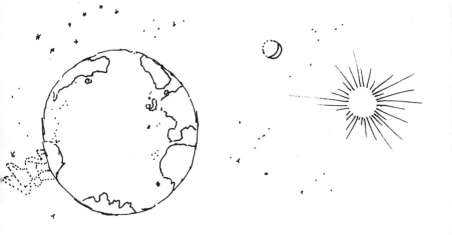

What is it like for you
when we ask you questions, Emmanuel,
and what is your work with us?

I enjoy your questions immensely,
because we come to the subtleties.
"Ah," I say, "now I remember the pleasure
of my humanness!"
When one digs deeply enough
into one's own life, one begins to discover
these frozen pieces of infinite knowing.

I hear your longings
and I celebrate your questioning,
for you bring me to the very center
of my purpose.
Every question is a doorway.
Some are wide and others narrow.
Some can admit only a tiny crack of light,
yet it is the beginning
of the opening of the door
and so we hail it with much love.

The moment that forgetting begins to question,
then forgetting will never be so dense again.
When you, in illusion, turn to ask,
"What else is there?"
then you are removing illusion.
What remains is eternity, perfect Love,
Beings of Light, Angels, your true *Selves*,
however it is you wish to express it.

*"There must be something more
than this" is the voice of Love.*

Let me suggest that you take back the power
which you all-too-willingly
accord the spirit guide.
We walk with you in Love,
but not with a bag full of tricks.
If you want to know something, try this:

*Sit quietly and tell yourself,
"I grant myself permission
to know what I know,
to see what I see,
to hear what I hear."*

If you can frame a question,
you already know the answer.

You in your form and we in ours
are moving to the same call of Love.
There is really nothing magical
about the means by which the world of spirit
and the world of human experience
mesh together. It is one
of the most ordinary and
yet unrecognized happenings.

I come to speak to you,
not of what *I* know, but of what *You* know,
not of who I am, but of who *You* are.
I come to the planet to assist at the birth
of your total and complete memory
as much as each human being will allow me.
I come to challenge you to your greatness
and your faith.
Let us explore together
not from the terror of forgetting,
but for the joy of remembering.

Your presence on this planet
is absolutely essential.
Not one of you is here by mistake.
There is Divine intent here.
You will ultimately transform the
Earthly illusion,
which you yourselves created,
back into Oneness.

*When the final soul
has satisfied its curiosity
and its noble purpose,
not only your planet,
but all the creatures that exist
under the heavens will,
with a glorious blaze of Light,
return Home.*

Will there, then, be nothing in the skies?
Will there be no sun, no stars, no planets?
Not unless you decide to create some more,
which undoubtedly you will.

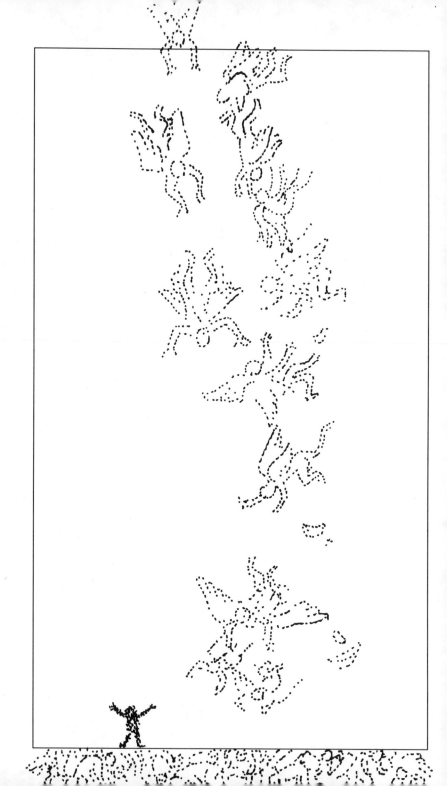

3
The Angel's Descent into Darkness

Your world is filled with Angels
who have lost their way,
who have forgotten who they are.

There is nothing that stirs an Angel
to leave the Oneness except the call of Love.
You are called into humanness again and again
by this voice and by the song
of your own heart as well.
You come bearing your special gift,
a wondrous message,
one flame of Light that is uniquely
and particularly your own.
As small children you knew that.

You are educated to illusion.
The things you are taught
are useful as tools for your journey,
but not for true self-identification.

The difficulty begins at the moment of birth.
As you move from the womb
into the human world,
you are surrounded by Angels.
The young child sees them.
(Isn't it poignant that people think
that a newborn baby cannot see clearly?
The truth is that the child can see more clearly
than perhaps ever again in life.)
Those Angels are gathered to promise the soul
that it will not be left alone,
and at the same time, to bid Godspeed.

This journey into unknowing is necessary.
You have come to explore the world of illusion.
If you still held the clear knowledge
of your true identity, you would merely
dance along the periphery of life,
never fully entering into it.
Illusion is created to serve Love,
and you are here to become part
of that human experience.

The human personality
devises such amazing disguises
for greatness to wear.

As small children,
you heard the winds of doubt
whistling around you
and you thought, "The only way
to keep my flame of remembering safe
is to put it inside my inner sanctuary,
close the door, and forget where it is."

To ease the pain of that conflict,
children determine to forget.
Your willingness to release
your memory of angelhood
is a choice.
I daresay every unhappiness,
every illness, every disappointment,
that you have encountered in your lives
comes from that awesome moment
when you decided to release the memory
of who *You* really are
and abide within the structures and strictures
of your human habitat.
The glory of your journey is forgotten.

Visions and dreams are bridges
between Angel and human.
They are the passions that compel you
forward into self-expression.
Where do you love yourselves the most?
Be there.
Can you know the one direct way?
I am happy to say that you cannot.
Your heart will call you
down the most surprising,
unique, and unexpected pathways.

The challenge is to dare to believe your dreams
in the center of illusion.
Take a long minute or two
and ask yourselves:

If I had it to do over,
what dream would I follow that I put away
for whatever hundreds of reasons?

What vision did I have?
What longing did I allow to be altered
out of recognition
by the demands of my life?

What voice called me
that I turned away from
because I felt
I had no right to follow it?

Should you find a glimmer of an answer,
let yourselves honor that lost grail.
However modest, impractical,
or even vainglorious the child's dreams
may have been,
they came from the deep inner memory
of perfect Love.

Do not test the validity
of your dreams
against the inconstancy
of illusion.

You live your human lives
in great loneliness, reaching out
to be filled by the sense of Oneness
you still hold in unconscious memory.
You lose your true *Selves* in childhood
through the reactions you learn
in order to survive in your world.
You look for your identity
in the way others respond to you
so that you can then adjust your way of being
in order to be loved.
You live by reflection.
You might now consider
that those same "others"
are looking back at *you*
to be their mirror.

You all carry murdered dreams
in your back pockets.
Those dreams are taken from you as children.
It is not that you are the victim
of some unmentionable cruelty,
for you must be helped
to enter fully into the illusion
if you are to taste the gamut
of human experience.

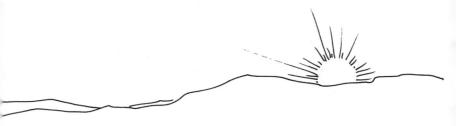

You attempt,
in the name of the Love that you remember
and in the name of the fear you hold,
to be who you "ought" to be.
You become immersed
in an ever greater pageantry of confusion.
Much of the time that feels comfortable
and familiar because your journey has, indeed,
taken you fully into the human world.

The mind, which is well equipped
to walk within the confines of the illusion
and wend its way from birth to death,
one day finds itself standing at the edge
of what seems to be a most dangerous precipice.
Mind realizes that it cannot understand,
cannot solve, nor can it control.
You experience a shriek of fear
that enters your lives and your bodies.
You become tense and anxious.
Often you become ill.

You ask yourselves,
"What is the matter with me?
Why am I not content?"
Your heart is whispering,
"Listen to me. This is not Home.
You did not come for contentment.
You came to remember."

At the golden moment when you are ready,
you understand that your quest
has really always been the search for *Self*
and for the lighted way Home.

When your remembering opens wide,
you will see nothing on your planet
that does not speak to you
of the fundamental nature of Oneness
that exists within the heart of every living thing.
Indeed, you will hear
the heartbeat of the planet itself.

You will recognize
that even this sheltering globe called Earth
knew all along what it was doing
when it agreed, "I will form myself
into an abundant garden
to circle through what seems to be
the vacancy of space.
Through all time I will cherish
the truth of our partnership
as I hold upon me the myriad pieces of Love."

**Does the Angel know what it is doing
when it is down in the darkness?**

The Angel inevitably is aware of all things
and is enjoying the journey tremendously.

So as the human experience
dwells on the sense of lostness,
the Divine Being simply walks
from place to place,
allowing the directives to be received,
knowing their Divine nature
and experiencing the absolute assurance
that no one is ever lost.

Just at the edge of the fingertip of breath,
the fog of shadowy human experience
begins to be blown gently away
by the whispers of truth
as they become more and more apparent
within the human awareness system.
These moments of greater recognition
become paramount in their importance
to the human life.

In the beginning,
you are wandering in what seems unmarked
and uncharted areas of darkness.
As the dawning of memory opens,
you find—placed most expertly—signs,
instructions, implications, urgings
that unfailingly direct you
to the next necessary and most worthy step.

These things can come in many different forms,
from something as insignificant
as tripping over a submerged rock
to a blatant neon sign flashing
the exact appropriate words to you
at exactly the appropriate moment.

Allow your lives the private assurance
that whenever you have a sense of wonder,
you will find—at the very edge
of the next moment of experience—the answer,
full-blown and generous,
waiting to be received by you.

**Why do some Angels in human bodies
have to suffer so much?**

From a human viewpoint,
any suffering is difficult.
One need only look around a small area
of your own towns and cities
to see unexplainable, unreasonable,
unconscionable suffering.
Do not allow your minds to lull you to sleep
by telling you, "Oh, well, it's this karmic device
or that spiritual lesson."

I promise you that there is a greater purpose,
but I also assure you that mind cannot know it.

*As long as you live,
you will never receive
satisfactory answers
to the why of suffering on your planet.
If you look back
on the challenging times
in your own life,
you can see the treasures they brought.
Let that be enough.*

**There seems to be a pervasive willingness
to lie in our society. Is this willingness to lie
at the root of the whole illusion?
Is the world a lie?**

Fear is the lie.
The world may be a place of badgering,
of pain, of cruelty.
Is that all it is? No.
It is also a place of infinite possibility.
It is a place where Angels come to walk
within the ranks of disbelief.

Everyone, no matter how roguish,
no matter how vicious or dishonest,
has the flame of their Divine being
alive within them.
The one who longs to alleviate the pain
on the planet asks, "Then how
can I reach that flame?"

By remembering your own.
Everyone longs to see the Light,
even as they sink deeper
into their own darkness and terror
and into their own reactions
to that terror
which are in themselves terrifying.

Can you remember how it was with you
when the despair became so great
that you had to move out, to break away?
Outrage stepped in to demand,
"Is there no justice?"

Not to satisfy the mind.
Is there no punishment? No.
In the broader concept,
human life is not about crime and punishment.
It is not about problem solving.
It is not even about rescue.
It is about remembering.
Fear cannot be your leader
because it can only take you deeper into darkness,
and you are not headed that way.

Injustice is terribly real
within the planetary experience.
Let your hearts break,
but do not abandon your life.

When the human witness to pain
is present,
then the compassionate Angel
is also there.

**Why does the illusion have to be so strong
and why is so much forgotten?**

You are excellent creators.
It took a great deal of ingenuity
to bring about this world,
where love seems not to be,
because your memories are strong
and your love connects you
with the world of Oneness.
It was necessary,
if you were to join the adventure at all,
to make the forgetting as profound as possible
and the illusion as "real" as could be devised.
Failing that, your world
would have no compelling nature.
It would be just a shadow.
Since your nature is Light,
how could you become disassociated
with that Light
if the darkness were not convincing?

So the Angel
must assume the wardrobe of illusion,
for the Angel
cannot leave the Oneness without it.
This will bring you to the exact depth
of forgetting which your soul has chosen.

*No matter how far one tumbles
into illusion,
one is still
in the center of Light.*

Is there any such thing
as a nonfragmented human being?
On the surface of things, there is not.
Every human being struggles
with the seeming gulf
between the profound wisdom of the soul
and the workings of the intellect.
At the same time, there is a meeting point,
and it is found within the heart.

Self-love is the key
to remembering your angelhood.
Embrace yourselves right as you are
at this moment with all of your pretense,
all of your confusion.
You have never done anything
that did not come from Love.
The six-month old infant
does not harbor sinister intent
with the thought, "All right, I'll try to be
who you want me to be."
That is the child's act of Love.

Here is a helpful practice:

Let yourself believe
that you have a right to love the self.
Love yourselves with an open heart
as long as you are able.
Then watch what closes the door.

How can we know our dreams in this illusion?

I return you to your visions,
hopes, and aspirations,
which are the things the Angel came to do.
What opens your heart?
Vocabulary and costumes of dreams
may spring from fear,
but not the essence of the dream.

You come at Love's call
and Love does not stop calling
because you put on a human body.
It calls all your life in many voices,
many forms, for different causes.
It is the Light you follow.

What you love to do most
is the shortest distance
between where you are now
and your dreams.

How can we know if our Angel guides are still there?

The only means of communication is Love.
In fact, the only means of existence is Love.
What you do to yourselves
throughout your days is not Love,
but to a great extent it is self-alienation.
So to hear us, to know we are there,
first hear yourselves
and know that *You* are there.

We do not leave you
when you turn again to blindness and deafness,
yet you believe that you are alone.
That painful experience
is at the core of the nature of illusion.

Please remember,
as you walk through your lives,
that although your breath of creation
and intent of perfection
may become grotesquely distorted,
everything you have ever done
has always been, at its inception,
an act of Love.

However,
the moment that the act is breathed into life,
fear rushes in to announce,
"I know what to do with that.
I have the structure right here.
This is your name.
This is your family history,
and this is what you do.
That is who you are.
Now, where were we going to put
this wonderful creation?"

4
The Fog
of Familiarity

You have been taught
that things are irrevocably written in the granite
of life's familiar guarantees.

Beware of the allure of the familiar,
for it will put you to sleep
quicker than any other lullaby.
The suppositions of a lifetime
enshroud you in limitation.
The world has taught you
appropriate thoughts and it has fostered opinions
and encouraged judgments
that you have inflicted upon yourselves
from the time you could think at all.
These demands lock you in prison.

You must inevitably
come to a point in your life
when you recognize that the forcing current
of demand comes not from a loving heart
but from a fearful head.

Mind is the instrument
of the human world,
not of eternity.

"What is the journey about?" you wonder.

I can tell you what the journey is *not* about.
It is not about being
whoever you were taught you ought to be.
It is not about obeying the histories
related by your well-meaning families.
It is not about the givens of the world.
It is not about conforming to a concept,
even such a concept as enlightenment.
Your lives are not about pleasing someone else.
This does not mean that you are thoughtless,
rude, arrogant, or lacking in compassion.
It means that you are who *You* really are.

As infants newborn you are all very wise.
Though you may have seemed to look around
with eyes still myopic
from intrauterine experience,
I promise you that you saw much more
than you do now. You saw essence.

~

Do not think,
you who are parents of young children,
that you have them fooled.
If they could speak, they would tell you
exactly who you are
in the most profoundly tender terms.
They would also be absolutely clear
about who *they* are and what they have come
to share with the human world.

Shortly after infancy,
children become enthralled
with the human experience,
and find themselves forgetting
they are Angels.
They believe they are toddlers.

Fear put in its appearance early in life,
but I am not making fear the arch-demon
of human experience,
for in the beginning it came at your request.
You said to fear,
"Let us devise, you and I,
a warning system
that will help avoid all pitfalls."

You and fear became partners—
but partners to the frightened child,
not to the adult seeking truth.

You have spent this present lifetime
searching for perfect Love.
You have looked to teachers,
to religions, to books, to ideas,
to philosophies, why, even to spirits,
and you have not yet found
the promise of that perfection—
because you have been looking
outside yourselves.
Such a Love awaits within you.

Do not look for Love where it cannot be found.
You will know the Love that you seek
when you turn to honor that true *Self*
you left at the doorway of your birthing.

How can I overcome my fear of Love?

The first thing you do *not* do
is turn and charge with guns blazing
and sabers unsheathed.
After all, the relationship with fear is so deep
that if, at some combative moment,
you destroy it, you destroy a portion
of your familiar self as well.

Fear of Love is the human condition.
It is not unique to you.
It is the causative factor in every life
that inflicts upon you loneliness,
self-denial, a suppressive self-control,
pain and sickness.

The natural Love within you
has been overlaid many times
with the dictionary of love
that you were offered by your world.
It is your definition of love
that is causing you to fear.

Explore your mind's dictionary of love.
Ask yourselves these questions.

What do I think Love is?
What are Love's demands?
What are Love's requirements?
What is Love's nature?
What do I want from Love?

The language of love you
were taught is the love you have lived,
yet the inner wisdom knows full well
that that is not who *You* really are.
One could say that you have been walking
in a well-intentioned charade
with your current definition of love
costumed in illusion.

Do not let mind
fashion the patchwork garment of your loving.
Whatever clothing you decide to wear each day,
make sure that there is a place on the sleeve
where your heart can be worn.

It seems a great risk
to release the beliefs of fear,
which seem to have kept you safe
all through life. Yet your heart
is calling you to say yes to Love.
Do not let fear weave tall tales
of what Love really is.
Fear does not know.
This very moment choose Love.
See what happens.

"What is this business of being human?"
you may wonder.
"Am I to go through the doorway
of separation into humanness
only to find, down the road,
that I am not even who I was taught
to believe I am?"

Yes, you are.

"The idea that I am not the familiar me
is more than a little disturbing," you say,
"Then what am I to do?"

Await each moment's arrival,
and when it comes to you,
greet it as though you have never seen it before,
for the truth is, you never have.
Ask yourself the questions
"What is Love doing here?
What is fear saying here?"
Allow neither Love nor fear to speak
under the umbrella of familiarity.

The false beliefs of your planet are many,
but there are only one or two that each one of you
has chosen to work with during this lifetime.
They are the pithy sayings of your historic family,
the givens with which you have grown up.
"The world is a dangerous place."
"Don't let your emotions show."
Here is some lifelong homework:

Look at these guidelines which you have
used to bring yourselves into the center of illusion.

When you find such dictums—
and you will surely do so
because you use them so often
that they have become as familiar as the air
you breathe—write them down.

Start a collection of them.
Then read them over and remind yourself,
"This is not eternal wisdom.
It's just some old superstitions from my family."

Even love's knowing must not be etched in granite.
Leave all doors and windows in the mind open,
for in the next instant love may surprise you
with another gift. Do not insist
that meanings remain the same today, tomorrow,
and twenty years hence.
You are always in a position to alter
your belief system.

You worry about your safety:
from death, from loneliness, from penury,
safety from the fear of fear itself.
There is a veritable cornucopia of reasons you
offer fear to justify its existence.

I want to ask you now:
what is it you really seek safety from?
Are you not essentially
seeking safety from the journey?
When one enters into life's school,
one must be willing to accept
the complete curriculum.
That does not mean that you are doomed
to suffer.

Then what is life supposed to be like?

There is a misrepresentation
about the meaning of life.
Fear informs you, "If you are going to be
human, this is what you will have to deal with:
loneliness, abandonment, and disappointment
at the very least.
If you allow yourself to live long enough,
you will have to deal with old age,
decrepitude, loss of mind, and all the rejection
society seems to inflict
upon that stage of the journey.

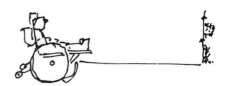

"In addition, you will have to deal
with not really ever being sure of anything.
You had better walk with me to keep safe,
and therefore you will also have to walk
with doubt and insecurity, and you'd best
walk very very carefully
to avoid chaos and terrible pain."

Well, when one has one's course description
put in such a way,
who indeed would want to matriculate?
"I will be different," you decide.
"I will specialize. I will look for safety first...
not for what gives me joy in my heart.
Then I can survive the awesome business
of living."

You begin to relax in the belief
that you have set it all up safely,
and then life comes crashing in.
Your first response is "What did I do wrong?"
Your second reaction is
"How dare life do that to me?
Here I had everything carefully planned out
with deep regard for my own tenderness
and feelings of inadequacy.
I had hoped to avoid certain things,
yet here they are, looming large before me,
and they won't go away."

This is all predicated on fear, dear ones.
There is nothing you cannot abide
in your human world.
If you walk with Love,
there is nothing that will cause you such distress.
Because you are afraid
does not mean that you are in danger.
It is time for you all to stop
believing fear's teachings.
Fear is the false prophet,
not a leader who will get you through the night.

The Light,
which is what You are,
can walk into the familiar human fog
or into the dungeons of hell
and still remain pure Light.

Fear seems to permeate
all aspects of your human world
for a while until you have determined,
"I won't let fear suggest what courses to take.
I'll just sign up for the entire thing
from beginning to end.
I can't avoid it, and I don't even want to.
Here I am."

The moment that "Here I am" enters,
you are home free, graduation guaranteed.

When I am in panic,
I find it difficult to focus on Love at all.
Is there a trigger to break the fear force?

Find one thing you trust as an amulet,
a reminder, something dear to you.
It could be a pet, a rock, an object of any sort.
It could even be a mantra or a poem.
Carry it in your heart if not in your hand.
In a moment of panic
when you believe you do not believe (for that is
where panic comes from),
find that special thing and focus on it.

Your mind will race.
You must stand fast: "No, I'm staying here where
I know there is truth
even though I cannot touch truth right now."

Let the tornadoes
of terror spin off into the distance.
Fear exists only when you feed it.
In those moments of terror,
trust your heart.

Does fear serve any useful purpose
other than to keep us away from tigers?

It keeps you alert within the world.
It keeps you riveted to the ongoing drama of life
with its repeated litany "Never sleep.
Never rest. Never believe."

Every time you are afraid,
see fear as a familiar outworn talisman.
It was the badge of familial allegiance
you were offered that admitted you
into the inner sanctuary of your home.
To remove that badge is not disloyalty.
It is the fulfillment of the promise.

Consider fear as the vestiges of history
clinging to your ankles as you attempt to climb
to the top of the mountain.
What would you do if you viewed fear
as just the vines of the past?
You would simply kick them away.

How does one rid oneself of fear?

Do not worship it.
When I remind you to choose Love,
I am saying to take off your blindfolds,
remove your costumes,
unwrap the shrouds that have kept you distant,
lonely and in pain,
and be present in this moment.
Choosing Love is saying yes to life.
Fear would advise you to say no.
You are faced with a choice.
"Are there no other alternatives?" you ask.

Fundamentally, there are no others.
Your choice is between illusion and truth.
There is no particular formula for choosing.
There is only your intent. Will that be enough?
It will be enough to start you on your way.

Keep asking yourselves, "Am I here now?"
Just that question
will make enormous changes in your lives.
If you ask it experientially
rather than philosophically,
you will find that it becomes a mantra
that will bring you back,
breath by breath, to this time, to this place,
for in truth there is no other.

As you set yourselves free from your histories,
you will wear your costumes more lightly;
you will smile much more than usual,
and you will release your hearts
to the point where you begin to trust them.
You will, in short,
let yourselves out of prison, bar by bar.

Fear is a habit.
As you recognize it,
you will be able to loosen the viselike grip—
not that fear has upon you—
but that you have upon fear.

Fear will go away
once you give it permission
to leave.

FEAR IS ILLUSION

That should be
on the first page of every dictionary.
Fear is illusion no matter how sensibly it is
defined, how historically it is verified.
There is nothing that can happen to you
which your soul
has not already endorsed.

Nothing can harm *You*.
You are eternal.

No matter what fear tells you,
it is never true.
Fear is blind and deaf.
It sees only its own expectation.
To realize that fear is illusion is
the beginning of freedom.
Once you know fear's nature,
then the next time it pays you a visit,
you will be able to say, "There's
that illusion of fear again.
I wonder what I have forgotten
this time."

*Be willing to walk five minutes of each day holding to
that statement.*

*In a week,
expand that period to ten minutes,
then twenty. Be patient.*

Even the most noble wonderings
of your fearful mind
are still the barrier
that keeps you from the fulfillment
that you would think yourselves into
if only that were possible.
How many years, how many lifetimes,
have you pursued intellectual understanding?
If we were to propose some formula
in which you could be simply present,
do you think you would be willing to do that?
The idea may seem paramount
in its importance to your well-being,
yet, I daresay, shortly the mind will be convinced
that though it all may sound like good idea,
it requires some thinking about.

*Do not plead the case of your life
to the tribunal of your mind.
It will keep you in court
for another six hundred years.*

Practice resting in this moment
without the need to know anything.

Go outdoors.
Imagine you have just been born.
You do not know what anything is.
You are introduced to everything right
in this moment with no previous experience.

Begin to touch the perfection and the magic
of this new world.
Do not judge anything as good or bad
but look to see the opportunities
for Love all around.

Every moment that you choose Love,
every second you allow your heart to open,
you transform not only your own life
with a sense of joy and purpose,
but you bring a great blessing to your planet.

Must children be willing to be abused
time and time again?
Must soldiers be willing to die?
Must people be willing to starve to death
somewhere for the ultimate awakening
of some one person who is vicious and cruel
and absolutely unlovable?

All Love is eternally magnanimous.
The answer is obviously yes.

I do not attempt to explain away
the pain of your planet by saying
that there is a greater cause.
I am saying that there is a greater cause,
so therefore *feel* this pain.
Is that not what tears are for?
Do not lose faith.

Let each tear wash away the fog.
They will not tarnish truth.

The challenge is to sit in the darkness
and believe in Light.
It is a journey worthy of the gods *You* are.
You did not come to tinker.
You came to explode.

Why am I so tired all the time?

The weightedness you all feel
is because you have accumulated what you believe
are so many requirements and obligations
that you have packed them into valises,
trunks, handbags, and backpacks.
You wear them, these invisible symbols of bondage.
You walk day by day fulfilling the expectation
that you have assumed.

Although you may seem to be victims
of your entire heavy history,
I assure you that you are not.
You are not victims of anything
except perhaps of your own reluctance
to move beyond the familiar.

Why are change and uncertainty so threatening?

The heart has a way of saying "I don't know
how I know. I just know."
This drives the mind to distraction.

This statement seems to offer you
the impossible choice of either going along
with the mind to calm it
and perhaps to give yourself a sense of belonging
in your world or following your heart
and risking...what?

One wonders what you are really risking.
Everything you do involves change.
You so often experience change
as though something terrible were happening
when in reality the change is moving you
from confinement into freedom,
from habit into truth.
Crossroads are the call to exploration.

What is a miracle?

It is the natural flow of Love's power.
It is the Angel present upon the planet Earth.
It is the Love that you feel in your own heart.

A miracle is mind's definition
for Love's natural capacity to be.

The mind sets up boundaries
of reasonable expectation and declares,
"This is the natural order."

Love enters and knows no boundaries.
The presence of Love,
which is indeed the only reality that exists,
takes all of mind's careful planning
and simply blows it to bits.

Mind has determined, "Reason comes to this point
and can go no further."

Love does not even see the barrier.
When Love crashes through
mind's familiar understanding
of how things "ought" to be,
mind can only cry out, "That's a miracle!"

"No," Love answers, "that's just the way I am."

5
Some Categories
of Human Confusion

Trust your intent, your journey,
your hearts, and your loving selves.

The only purpose for questions
is to help you become more comfortable
with the wisdom you already own.
Your questions are really fear asking,
"Do I have a right to know what I know?
Does it fit into the limited self
I was taught to believe was necessary?"

That is an appropriate belief
for the journey into illusion,
but once you have turned to seek the Light,
the old beliefs no longer serve.
Let them fall away.
It is astonishing how fond you have grown
of your old jail cells.

**Often the demands of everyday life
interfere with time with family
and other matters of utmost importance.
How do I best support myself and my family
and still remain my Angel?**

Your question
is predicated on the misconception
that when you are busy in your human world
and devoting your attention
to the endless demands of human experience,
you are not your Angel *Self*.
Perhaps you believe that your Angel
is sitting on a cloud or stored in a closet
waiting for the busyness to be done with
so that there can be "Angel time."

The truth of the matter is
that your entire life consists
of nothing but Angel time.
Do Angels rush to get to work?
Evidently they do.
Do Angels become profoundly engrossed
in the day-to-day discontent, confusions,
and problem solving of their families?
Indeed, yes.
It is the illusion of separation
that spawns the question.
The Angel is always there under the most raucous
of circumstances, in the center
of the most compelling domestic chaos,
because the Angel is *You*.

Please help me.
I have been feeling crushed
so often these days
with the blackest despair.

The nature of despair is not really who you are.
I am not going to talk you out of it.
I would, if I could, talk you into it.
Despair, pain, and grief are held to be unpleasant
and thoroughly undesirable.

Dearest friend, take the lighted candle
of your own faith, and enter completely
into your despair.
Be there. Look around.
Let your self-remembering light that cavern,
demanding nothing, expecting nothing.
Rather than push away your despair,
just say yes to it.

If you are in your despair, an Angel is there.
If you say yes to your pain,
then that pain is filled with Love.
This is not something to think or merely perform.
It is something to *be*.
Say yes in that despair-filled moment
when you are able,
and with your next breath say yes again.
Let the breath that follows also be a yes.
And, if you are willing to allow
the structure of despair to alter,
you will observe it beginning to change.
You are in no danger.

My mother is old and her husband is ill.
My grown unmarried son is unhappy.
I am staying married
to a woman I don't love for their sakes
and because I do not care to meet anyone else
at this time. How can I help myself cope
and learn unconditional Love?

You describe yourself
in terms of human permission.
"What am I to do?" you ask.
"This is all dependent on me.
How can I choose self-love
when so many require that I do not?
Do I have a right to live my own life?"

Let me tell you a story.
Many eons ago,
You came into the presence of God.
Describe it in your mind in any manner you like.
You said, "I am going on a journey.
I am going out into the void
and I am going to fill it as I go
with whatever I am,
whoever I am, in that moment.
I will be like a star shooting out into the darkness
of yet-to-be, and as I move,
my very presence will create."

So you began your journey,
and you have touched countless realities
as you have floated, soared, and crashed
through the yet-to-be-created areas of eternity.
With every moment of your presence,
new things have come into being.

Right now, in this particular life,
nothing exists beyond the moment.
The next moment awaits your creation.
With your next inhalation,
you bring forth whatever you allow
through the composite performance
of what you have already created,
what you allow to be present now,
and the capacity for Love you choose.

As you walk your life,
remember you are an Angel.
You are quite literally a comet of consciousness
that creates where it passes,
but where it has yet to be has not been formed.
Do you believe that the highways upon
which you drive your car
are simply laid out without your presence?
Do you believe that the events that you
are going to experience during the rest of your life
are already somewhere waiting for you?
Nothing happens until you get there,
rather like the honored guest at a surprise party.

Now, to your question.
Your mind tells you, "I must stay
for those who are so dependent on me."

How can you be sure of that?
You cannot possibly know what bounty
you will bring to those whom you believe
require your presence until you say,
"I am listening to my own inner voice
and taking Love by the hand.
I am going to honor who I am."

Fear warns, "You will cause untold suffering
and the heavens will fall."

Nonsense.
Doors will open.
Do you think you fool people
with performance?
What you give in sacrifice
is not a gift at all but an IOU which states,
"See here, I've done my duty as expected."
The bookkeeping continues.
Resentment builds.

These books can never be balanced.
Nor do they need to be.

Many of you wish
I would give you some kind of data system
wherein you enter the facts and receive a printout
of what to do,
but I am delighted to say I cannot.
You are committed to living your lives,
believing that you are in error at moments,
and at all times offering yourselves
the Divine choice for self-love.

**Some people use drugs to get to a place
they think of as more spiritual,
more outside the bounds of human limitation.
Is that ever a worthwhile way
to try to touch the angelic?**

For some it may be the only way.
What makes it not worthwhile
is that chemicals carry with them
the heaviness of the Earth.
Therefore, though they may activate
certain glandular release within the human body
so that the terrestrial deafness and blindness
seem to dissipate for a short while,
they also bring with them the promise
that the door will close again.

If a drug is used more than once or twice,
it causes dependency to elicit the opening,
so it offers a false lure that tells you,
"You cannot get there unless you take me."
That is unfortunate,
since what for a moment was a release
to see beyond the blindness
becomes the densest of blindfolds,
enslaving you more deeply.

Is it ever useful? When one is hopeless,
any light is useful.

I have been wanting a soul mate
for a number of years.
I deserve it.
I am ready for it.
Perhaps I don't believe it.
Can you help?

What does "soul mate" mean?
To some it means a perfect companion
to walk with for the rest of your life,
someone who is the most wonderful provider,
lover, and, perhaps, fixer of leaky faucets.
What does the word mean really?
Everyone you have ever loved is a soul mate.
Everyone upon your planet is a soul mate,
even those who are official rascals
or profoundly despairing images
of destruction.
Everyone who is in your consciousness
now is a soul mate.
I do not mean to trivialize your question,
but to spread it to its greater truth.

You reach to another with the false expectation
that others can fill you.
They cannot.
It is a joyous experience to walk hand in hand
with another human being whom you love,
but if you are both empty,
if you have not filled yourselves
with your own devotion,
then you begin to lean on each other
and demand something that is impossible
for any other human being to supply.

Make room in your life
for the ordinary sweet human beings
all around you who will give you the opportunity
to practice giving and receiving Love.
Let your heart learn loving.
You cannot keep the door closed
until the perfect one appears.
That "one" only walks through
already opened doorways.

How do I reduce stress?

Learn to trust who you are.
Give yourself the day, or two days.
I promise you
that if you give yourself permission to stay in bed,
doing nothing, you will be up
and doing what you love
by ten o'clock and you will not be stressed.

Stress comes from the internalized tyrant
who intones the mantra
of your life, "You will not do it right.
You are not good enough."

Do you see why we say it is time
to fall in love with yourselves?
Does an Angel require scolding?
Use meditation as an oasis
in the confusion of your days.
Try this brief attunement to the *Self.*

Take a moment to get quiet.

Then imagine that the crown chakra,
the opening at the top of your human physicality,
begins to soften, to expand.
This part of your being allows for the world of spirit
to emerge and then flow back again
into your humanness as you fall asleep
and awaken, or as you meditate,
and as you love.

Breathe up and down through the
crown opening.

As you go about the rest of your day,
bring your attention briefly
to the crown of your head.
Remind yourself that nothing matters
to the extent that fear has convinced you it does.

When a small infant is formed,
nothing, at the moment of birth, is solidly based.
The top of the head is open.
I know you cannot walk around
in your adult lives
with your physical brains covered
only by a membrane,
but would it not be excellent if you could live
your adult lives acknowledging the necessity
for that much room for growth?

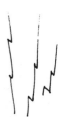

Do not see yourselves as solid.
Do not let your costumes bind you,
but always leave a great seam
in various points of your physicality
where unknown creation can take place.

Fear is terribly stressful. Truth is not.

**How can I get past my fear of expressing myself
and get in touch with my creativity?**

First, by not demanding that your creativity
be an obvious expression that others observe.
Begin gently to express yourself to yourself.
It can be a secret.
Give yourself permission
to be a closet creator for a little while.

Who are you trying to please
with your creativity? Are you giving it away?
Of course you are. If you were not,
you would be giving it to yourself
and you would enjoy it immensely.
You belong to you.

Birds do not sing so that others will applaud.

I understand from other enlightened beings
that part of why we are here is for self-purification.
Is this true?

If you are using the term "self-purification"
in place of "self-love," perhaps you are right.
The Angel does not come for purification,
but human beings cannot find the Angel
if they believe they are not worthy
of angelhood.
Until you can fully
and completely acknowledge who you are
and honor yourselves,
you cannot believe what I am saying to you.
You will continue to think
that there is something to be dusted or polished,
something that needs to be atoned for,
and on and on.

You do not come
from perfect Love, to be purified.
As a human being, you forget
and as you forget,
you become increasingly dense,
more aligned with matter than with truth.
As you begin to lighten the density of matter
and throw off the weights of illusion,
then one might possibly speak of purification.
One could also say, as I have done,
that you are here for remembering.
Trust that.

View yourself as a cake just mixed
and newly put into the oven.
You do not poke and prod the cake
to see how it is coming along.
Once the ingredients are stirred in
and the correct temperature applied,
then one must leave the rest
to the inevitable organic process.

Emmanuel, please speak regarding the experience
of "The Dark Night of the Soul," when a being has awakened
to Divine essence and then finds himself in despair
and doubt when the outer reflections of illusion
seem to have triumphed. Now the being
feels small and hopeless and overwhelmed.

As long as you are human,
you are bound to doubt.
Doubt is fear socially dressed.
Oh, I know there have been compelling times
when you are absolutely sure.
"Yes! This is it!" you said in moments of clear,
undeniable memory.
At other, dimmer moments,
you wring your hands and lament,
"How many times do I have to know the truth
before I can let go of doubt?"

The number is uncountable.

What causes The Dark Night of the Soul
is self-blame.
"Wait a minute. I went through all that,"
you say, "Why am I doing this again?"

It does not mean that you are bad.
Just human.
Self-castigation demands to know how,
if you were once blessed
to touch the Holy Grail,
you could have been so clumsy as to drop it?

I feel something like a wound in my heart area.
I can't seem to heal it.

Some of you insist on bringing forth
into the next incarnation a most recent injury,
not because you pledge
any particular loyalty to it,
but because it is the most direct route
back into illusion. For instance,
if you die from a spear wound to the heart—
and that is the master illusion
and at the same time the doorway
though which you have exited—
it remains a most handily available means
by which to become wrapped
in the schoolroom again.

When you construct your physical bodies,
you create within them every possible resource
both to enter illusion and to find truth.
When there seems to be some genetic weakness,
a mysterious malady,
it is one of those fail-safe devices
that you have interwoven
into your human vehicles
to sound the alarm when forgetting thickens
or the turning of the corner is imminent.
Nothing is wrong. The wound
does not have to be deliberately healed.
It has already served to bring you
into this moment of questioning.

Emmanuel,
how should we interpret our sleeping dreams,
and what is the real purpose of having them?

To a great extent,
they are indicative of what is awake
beneath the sleeping mind.
There are many layers of dreaming.
I would like to address a few.
The most obvious is the electrical discharge
from a busy day in which one seems to replay,
in some distortion, the events that took place
in the last twenty-four hours.
These are simply the releasing
of accumulated energy and need not be seen
as necessarily profound.

There is another layer of the dreaming state
when one begins to hold discourse
with suppressed material,
forgotten memories, when one begins to touch
the edge of one's truer *Self*.
From these dreams great wisdom can arise,
always and ever in the symbology
that would keep the mind at peace
while the message is imprinted on the heart.

To analyze your dreams, I suggest
that you rely more heavily on your intuition
and much less on the intellect.
Hear the full extent of your visions,
not just the voices caution has allowed.

Then there are dreams that go much deeper.
They do, indeed,
touch the core of the human being.
These dreams are recognizable
by their simplicity and by their profound effect
when you awaken. Utilize these
as you would any message from a place of wisdom.

There are also times
when you leave your physical bodies
and come Home for a visit.
Ask to be taken there the next time
you feel tired and discouraged.
You will awaken refreshed.

When I was young
my Siamese cat was a dear friend to me.
Often now I sense her presence and guidance.
Is this her love I carry with me?

One of the many wonders of your planet
is that Love comes packaged
in so many and such different shapes and sizes.
One of the most compelling
and available packages of Love
is animals,
particularly those who adopt you as pets
and warm your heart.
One such package could be a delightful cat.
Another might be a friendly dog
or even a bird that sings to you
once as you pass by.
Sometimes, believe it or not,
Love is a mosquito,
alighting upon your hand
and asking you for generosity.

Is the consciousness of Love that appeared,
in part, as your beloved cat still with you?
If it pleases you to think of that Love
in the form of a cat, it is quite all right.
It is not, however,
the form that brings the Love.
It is Love that brings the form.

Your cat
did not come as a separate piece of Love.
She came as a mirror.
"Well here *You* are in cat form," she says.
"How do you like it?"

Can you tell us what happens to an animal spirit after death?
Are our spirits one and the same?

Animals come to you as gifts,
as pieces of the *Self*
that you have strewn across the galaxies.
When you look with Love upon anything,
know that it is simply self-recall.
At the moment of recognition
you bring that piece of illusion back
into the truth of your own heart.

You come to the human planet
to bind into One the illusion of shattered *Self*.
Love is the only thing that can do that.

What happens to animal spirits after death?
They purr, bark, or roar themselves
back into the Light.

**Do all living organisms, whether dinosaurs,
human beings, mildews, or viruses
have a spiritual side to their makeup?
Do human beings have a special niche?**

The essence of all created things
is spirit, Light.
It is perfect and abiding truth,
from the minutest up to the grandest,
from an unseen virus
to the vastest reaches of space.
It is all of the same fabric.
It is all eternal and perfect Loving truth.
Creation takes countless forms
and will forever do so.

Are some things held in lesser merit
in the world of spirit than you are?
No.
You are all the same.
Perhaps you look down
upon a beetle in the grass and think,
"Well, surely I am more important than that."

Of course, you have no idea
of what is going on inside the beetle
and how it is regarding you.

How can we work with physical pain?

Pain did not come to be your enemy.
It may be hard to love,
yet it is there for your embracing.
Pain is a teacher and not to be feared.
Hear it as the voice of loving truth
telling you, "Wake up and pay attention now."

Get to know pain by holding it in your awareness.

See the cells of your body not as solid matter
but as molecules
separated by the spaciousness of your being.
You are consciousness.
You are Light inhabiting physical form.

See pain not as a solid block of immutable agony
but as pieces of **Self**
spinning in the immensity of the Light
that You *are.*

Soften. Inhabit the pain with Love.
Soften more.
Let yourself walk within that pain
in your inner vision
and touch most gently
each part of that discomfort.

When you feel familiar with pain,
begin to hold dialogue with it and ask
"Why have you come?
Have you a message for me?"

**Is there such a thing as spiritual death
and God's eternal damnation?**

There is not.
Can you see the falsehood in the idea
that the Eternal could turn away from Itself?
If there is such a thing as perfect Love,
then how could Love be destroyed?
Nothing has the power to damn a soul.

If fear tells you
that the Almighty Power can do this,
one wonders what kind of power
could that be which would take
a beloved piece of Itself and cast it out.
You yourselves, in your humanness,
know that the only way to transformation
is Love.
One does not chastise one's distortions.
They only become more embedded
in the illusion of rejection.
One embraces that which is in pain and,
by that Love, it is restored to its true nature.

You have all attempted
to damn and cast out parts of yourselves.
You believed that these parts
rendered you unfit to be loved.
That is fear's definition.
It does not survive one instant beyond
the barriers that illusion has erected
against the Light.

Is spiritual truth open for argument?
Dear heaven, has humanity argued
about anything else?
Have not wars been fought, murders committed,
enslavement enforced
because of a firm and arrogant misunderstanding
of the message from spirit?

**Are there alien forces that can harm our planet,
forces that the spirit realm cannot interfere with?**

No.
But I would like to suggest, most kindly,
that every one of you is an alien force,
since this is not your home.
To the extent that you forget who you are
and fall into the abyss of pain,
you, too, seem to become the agents
of unloving action.
Does that mean that your essence is unloving?
No. Just frightened.

Are there beings outside physical form
that can inflict themselves
upon your human planet?
Absolutely not.
The stories of dark beings, negative spirits,
hauntings, possessions, and all the horrifying
and at the same time titillating tales
of how dark darkness can become
are to be perceived with no more believability
than anything else that fear has taught you.

The truth is always brighter, clearer, cleaner,
and more loving than anything fear champions.

There are no dark spirits.
There are frightened human beings
who perform unloving acts.
Beyond illusion there is always truth,
and truth consists of one thing only—
perfect Love.

**What was the meaning
of the recent hurricane that terrified us?**

Trust a hurricane to know
where it is needed and how it can serve.
There is a compelling nature to such a storm
that brings everyone's attention
full focus on the moment.
Such a circumstance
seemingly opens the doorway to hell,
but what it really does is just open the door.
"Are you there now?" the hurricane roars.
"Are you there and what are you doing?
Do you choose Love? "

The Divine Plan will be carried out
sometimes in the most amazing
and even distressing manner.
From within the human experience
you cannot know the overall design.
The mind asks, "Why, why, why?"
I can answer only, "Because, because, because..."

You do not have to solve your lives.
You have only to live them.

I can promise you something.
There will come a moment,
perhaps beyond the grave,
when you look back
and see that from that monstrous storm
a tiny jewel of Light appeared.
Was it worth it?
Yes.

Has there been any improvement
in the level of consciousness
in our world in this century?

There is a movement to Oneness.
Can you believe that?
When you see countries proclaiming themselves
separate nations again, you say,
"But where is the Oneness there?"
It will come.

The events of the last fifty years
have brought about an astounding evolution.
People are waking up, some more slowly than others.
You no longer believe
that you can live in isolation.
You no longer assume that only the gifted
and talented can rule the world.
You no longer think
(though this is fading very slowly)
that might makes right.

There is a growing cognizance
that it is unacceptable
when someone is in pain,
when someone is alone,
when someone is starving
or has no place to sleep.
Child abuse can now be discussed.
Alcoholism and drug addiction
are being treated caringly and openly.
Look to see what really has come to pass.

Look at your own lives.
Notice what is taking place
in every part of the world.
There is disruption because there is change.
Freedom is dawning.
With the dawning of this freedom comes
disharmony and economic stress.

Now, what shall we do with this world?
You look around and you hear wondrous things
that cause you great enthusiasm,
and in the next moment
you hear of some terrible, unforgivable action
that causes untold suffering.
You see homes of delightful beauty and luxury
and in the next minute you turn
to find someone sleeping on the street.
You leave a restaurant
where you have had a sumptuous meal,
and you notice hungry children walking by you.
What does one do in a world of such duality?

The mind staggers.
It bombards you with suggestions.
"Mind your own business. That has
nothing to do with you."
"Let's run and hide before
they take something from us."
Or it might say, "The only thing to do
is to give away everything you own
and then perhaps some people will spend a night
or two in greater comfort."
"Let us march on government.
Let us raise the roof with our indignation
so that they (whoever 'they' may be
at that moment) will come to see,
understand, and do something about it."

You are all loving beings.
You perceive the pain and suffering
and you wonder, "What can I do?
I can't even do anything about my own."

When you choose fear and aversion
in a world of duality,
you add to the darkness of your planet.
When you choose Love,
your entire planet is lighter.
This affects everyone.
Your costumes may represent separation,
but your hearts do not.

What can the role of members of the media be?

Communication has come a long way
since the first grunt became a sound
that could repeat itself
with more or less the same meaning.
If you believe what eyes are taught to reveal,
you see nothing
but the fragmented human experience.
If you were to perceive the world
through the lens of the heart, however,
there would never be a sight, sound,
smell, or taste that would seem
other than All-That-Is.

Interpretation
through the usual channels of communication
has severed each one of you
from the wisdom and glory,
not of your past, but of your eternal present.
I do not want to imply
that the written or spoken word is the enemy.
If such communication
can come from the fullness
of an open and loving heart,
there is the possibility of communicating,
not differences, but sameness;
not separation, but Oneness;
not fear, but Love.
This message cannot move through
the editorial equipment
of those who are afraid.

In every moment of human experience
there is a gem of Love.
Even where fear is present
there is always and ever
the groundwork of truth.
There is nothing upon the planet
that does not hold the greater Design.
Knowing this,
perhaps you will deem it appropriate
to shift your focus
from the embattled human world
to the remembering of what is really there.

**Some of the great teachers who have been in human form
have taught their followers how to pray.
Is there a new way to pray today?**

There is.
You have been taught to pray
to a greater reality outside the self.
By that very act of projecting your Love
and longing outside the self,
you delay the moment of self-remembering.

Prayer is comforting.
It fills the ache of loneliness.
That is valuable and sometimes necessary
when fear is so convincing
that you truly believe that you are alone.

Prayer is not supplication.
Supplication removes you from the God within.
True prayer is the communication
with a deeper remembering inside the self.
The new way to pray would be to love.
Until you love yourselves absolutely,
you cannot remember who *You* really are.
Once you come into the memory of who *You* are,
prayer becomes a discussion
between comrades in spirit.

If there be any supplication in your prayer,
let it be that the Beings of Light around you
help you release yourself
from your limiting
historic definition.
Ask to be as present as possible
in this moment of eternity.
You are not only *in* eternity.
You *are* eternity.
You are not only *with* God.
You *are* God.

Why is the Bible so often used
as the absolute and only word of God?

Let me take you back in history a bit.
Spirit has spoken to your world
thousands of times.
How could it not, for your world of illusion
is held in the loving hands of eternal Truth?
When those brilliant moments come,
humanity (and fear) says,
"Let us take this moment of inspiration
and let us be very sure that no one forgets it."

It seems to be an act of Love
when man builds monuments
to make sure the truth is honored.
Yet if one can truly hear the voices of inspiration,
one must also know that such voices
will never vanish.
The connection in Love's name
holds through eternity.
Those special moments that the Bible
seeks to bring forth, therefore,
have been written, for the most part,
in the name of fear.

Remember that fear also knows
the vocabulary of Love.
Fear believed that the Being of Light
would not be remembered
and therefore His memorial had to be frozen
into the written word.
The human mind answers,
"Well, Emmanuel, people do forget."

They do.
People also die and yet the wisdom remains.
Christ was crucified
yet He still walks the Earth.
The truth of that life,
championed and celebrated, lives forever.
If there were no written texts of any faith,
do you truly believe that humanity
would forget God?

There are acts of Love in the Bible
that you hear metaphorically.
Hear them as fact.
Can human beings move mountains?
If they believe they can.
You created those mountains in the first place.
Can a sea be parted? Of course.
Was it? Do you dare to believe it?
Can a human being be nailed to a cross,
die, be brought down, buried,
and then rise again?
Fear tells you, "We have to temper this,
adjust it to where it is intellectually acceptable."

As you try to soften truth,
you bring yourselves farther
and farther away from Home
and the remembering of who *You* are
so that you walk in your narrow world
looking for proof that there really is a God.

Is truth so particular
that there is only one gate to heaven?
There are no gates.
Heaven is inside you.
You are not even the gatekeeper.

6
The Transparency of Darkness

Anything that brings you to your truth
is a blessing.

You all sit in a shower of Light,
wondering why it is dark.
It is your minds that rummage around
in the vast dictionaries of history
to research the word "Light."

The fundamental purpose of life
is not just to be comfortable
or to feel safe.
Passage into seeming darkness
involves pain, suffering, chaos.
Having duly arrived in the darkness,
it does seem that many are content
to remain there. That is because
they are too frightened to move.
They believe that if they hold their breath and endure,
it will go away.

In every soul's journey there must be a moment
when the question is raised:
"What is this all about?"
It is at that precise moment
that the Light is available.
In this way suffering serves a noble purpose.

What sense does it make for a child
to suffer invasive and painful medical procedures,
only to die of cancer?

Some Angels come as gifts to medical science.
Science holds good intent.
Many doctors are sincere seekers of
truth exploring the nature of life and death.
Who would not support such investigation?
Many doctors are really seeking God,
although they may not think of their quest
in those terms.

Those children
come in the name of Love
to say, "I will let you put into my body
whatever you think will rescue
thousands of others,
so do your invasive surgery."

In your compassion,
you want to cry out, "In the name of God,
take out the tubes, put down the scalpel,
cast out the poison, and let this child
live out the next three months in peace."

Fear is demanding, "We must do something
or this child will die."
Will the medical profession one day
cease to listen to the voice of fear?
Yes, and when fear's voice is silenced,
the enormous mill of pharmaceutical production,
too, will be all but stilled,
limited, perhaps, to gentle painkillers.
This will not be soon because death
is still the enemy in the temple
of which you speak.

What can I tell a friend who has AIDS?

Remind your friend that he is an Angel,
and that he has come to the planet
to bring the Light of who *He* is.
Illness will come and illness will go.
Is that not the nature of the human immune system
whether it is under attack or not?
That someone has been diagnosed with AIDS
does not mean they cannot heal
to reach a plateau of satisfactory function.
Tell your friend that he does not have to die
to earn the right to be alive.

A magnifying glass
has been turned upon the immune system
of those who suffer AIDS.
Do some die? Yes.
Will all of them die?
Not if they can be rescued from the false tenet
that once they have contracted AIDS
they are doomed.
Without a belief in that death sentence,
healing becomes more possible.

With normal life expectancy?

One wonders what normal life expectancy is.
If one lives with AIDS long enough,
the body's own resistance will create
an alternate immune system
which will then render
the attacking virus powerless.
What is required is enough time,
enough strength, and enough belief.
It is at the very beginning of the infection
that all of the effort must be made.
That will allow the immune system
to sustain itself and therefore
build its capacity to become stronger
when the next assault comes.

The body is rendered all-empowered
when the synchronicity of the physical,
emotional, mental, and spiritual are completed.
The initial viral assault can then be repelled
and there can be a peaceful coexistence
within the body's immune system
between the virus and the cells of the body.

AIDS comes as a stern teacher.
It rather walks around the classroom
as an old schoolmaster might,
and raps you smartly on the knuckles
saying, "Wake up!"

Illness is not a force
to pull one out of life.
Indeed, it is an invitation
to be in the center of one's life.

I work with patients who are diagnosed with
multiple personality disorder.
Can you discuss this?

It is a quagmire of seemingly unremitting suffering
for someone who has been so confronted
by harsh experience
that they must fragment themselves
in order to remain whole.
That sounds like a contradiction, but it is not.
A human being can fragment
so that what is believed to be overpowering
and absolutely crushing, unbearable suffering
can be dispersed.
One bit of pain can go to this personality,
another to that.

This provides space to breathe and become,
in each shard of that fragmentation,
a believable whole.
This is not a foolish means
by which to address the unbearable.
It is a most worthy and ingenious
means of survival.

The question arises,
if things are so difficult for some
that they must separate themselves
from the center of their being,
why would they want to survive?
Because they still struggle to be present
tells us that they are not completely separated,
that these fragmented selves hold enough
of the essence of the core
to allow for the viability of a human life.

In treating them, it would be useful
for you to create an area where each of the personalities
can be led to find its central theme
without as yet attempting
to relate to the whole.
To treat each emerging personality
with respect does not mean
that you will give it such validity
that it will remain separate.
You will give it comfort and safety
so that it can ultimately merge
again into the core.
That merging will automatically take place
as the central essence of each character is found.

Look for the core.
Look for the truth, the Love.
Look for the Angel.
If you listen intuitively,
you will begin to hear
the sweet and tender music of their wholeness.
When that becomes apparent,
you need only offer it back to them.
These shattered personalities
are looking for a place to call home.
They will gladly return to the central being
of the Angel-human if they can remember
that it is there.

Every one of you holds
the capacity for many different personalities.
We call them "costumes,"
and you change them with great rapidity.
In the human world
that is termed "healthy adjustment."
You are not the same person at a ball game
as you are in a ball gown.
You speak and act differently
with a maiden aunt than you do with someone
with whom you are cavorting
in a romantic spot.

It is a graphic display
when someone who has been released
from the compactness of the human personality
explodes into fragmentation
so that the pieces can clearly be seen.
Utilize this as a means of study
so that all human beings can see more clearly
how many hats they really wear.

**I was ritually abused as a child.
What should I do about it?**

Some Angels enter into human life
with a profound and seemingly
disturbing commitment
to go into the very bowels of forgetting
and to bring the Light of their innocence
into a darkness that can neither see
nor hear that innocence.
The Angel knew the journey.
The human child did not.

Let us recognize that an Angel,
knowing the nature of the chosen journey,
can walk through such a life and emerge
at the other side unscathed.
The child cannot.
There is anger, rightly so,
but did you come to know the darkness
and punish it, or did you come to bring Light?
Does one take revenge as one's purpose
and by so doing lash oneself to the mast
of the ship of darkness?
Did you not come to walk in your own Love?
That does not mean the abuse was all right.
Since there is no way to alter it at this point,
no purpose would be served
by clambering back into the dungeons of history.

Perhaps now you might begin to open doors
and windows, speak out and help others
explore such experience so that they
do not have to endure similar defilement.
There are many who would welcome
your intervention

**I want to see the Light in all parts of my life.
I feel I should forgive my father, who was cruel to me,
and yet I cannot. Could you discuss this?**

Forgiveness
is one of those highly charged words.
The definition you were taught
required you to say "It's all right"
when you felt hurt.
You believed that you had to go against your history,
abandoning the child that you were.
You renounced all hope of justice
on your human planet.
In speaking of forgiveness, then,
is it any wonder that your defenses go up quickly?

Let us change the meaning of forgiveness.
As long as you are allied with the belief
in the necessity of redressing wrongs,
you are indeed burdened.
Releasing history is not to let your father
go unpunished. Have more faith
in the nature of every human being.
No one escapes himself.

Forgiveness is not for another. It is for you.

**Should we allow another to harm us
and just turn the other cheek?**

That is one of the teachings that has come
to your world in the last two thousand years.
Does it mean that you are intended to be a victim?
No.

What is personal victimhood?
It is to be rendered powerless,
to yield to the will of another.
If you give over your power of self-love to another
and say, "You are the reason for my pain,"
have you not offered them your life?

There are many
whom you hold culpable in your lives
who have no idea that they have wronged you.

**Then how do we respond to the upraised fist,
the striking club?**

Fear would goad you into battle.
What would Love say?
See such behavior as a cry for help.
Send a blessing to the hearts of those troubled beings
who are so angry, so terrified.
They have yet to hear the voices of Love calling
and yet they, too,
came in the name of that call.

But what do we do with our fear and anger?

When you feel afraid and angry, try this:

*Close your eyes and go within. Search your own life
until you find one circumstance or one person
whom you do not want to love.
Do not scold yourself for it.
It is just part of the fabric of illusion.
Where is there one circumstance
from which you want to wring justice?
Where your heart closes?
Where your rage mounts?
Where your compassion balks? Find one.*

*Now let it stand before you for a moment.
Ask your heart, "Is this human being, this circumstance,
also held within the embrace of God?"*

Let your heart answer, not your mind.

*If you find that it is within God's embrace,
let yourself receive the lightness of that.
What has it cost you to carry this rage?*

Then allow your imagination, an excellent tool for truth,
to envision yourself taking this entire circumstance
and just dropping it down before you like a bundle.

"No, thank you," you say,
"I don't want to carry it anymore.
I want that particular pain out of my life."

Stand back and take stock now of how you feel.
Ignore the mind which, of course,
is simply waiting
for you to get through this exercise
to pick up the weight again.

What is the truth of you doing now?
Is it rejoicing?
Maybe it wants to tear this weighted thing
you have been carrying into colorful confetti
and toss it to the heavens.

Be surprised at nothing Love does.

**Can someone who has committed rapes,
murders, torture, suddenly awaken,
repent, and all that darkness is forgiven?**

Yes.
The mind reels at such sloppy bookkeeping.
"But what about the ripples of suffering
that human being has caused?"

The suffering caused
will wend its way to some good purpose
within the lives of those who are affected.
This does not mean that murderers must be allowed
to go about their murderous business
until they see the Light,
but neither does it mean that they must be treated
as though they are not Angels.

In just a single instant of awakening
the Angel is present,
and the universe gathers around to serve it.

Everyone on this planet
does the best he or she can
in any given moment.
Look around and you see the insanity,
the cruelty, the destruction.
Do not judge it,
but know compassionately that
whatever the results,
each person is operating
from the language of love he was taught.

The villain is the Angel
probing illusion
until he hits the wall of truth.
Honor the villain too.

Does it mean that you applaud the deed? No.
If the best thing you can do is to stop an injury,
then you do so.
If the best you can do is to tremble in a corner,
then that is what you do.
In retrospect,
you might, perhaps, make changes,
but that is mind's game.
It is not the heart's truth.

See nothing in your lives as meaningless.
The fact that no one really dies
does not make war right.
The fact that no one is surprised
by his own death
does not condone an assassination.

What *you* do in your human life
is profoundly important—
to you.

It is time you knew your good intent.
It is to do the best that you can do
in the name of the Love
you know you are.

What about the role of karma?

Let me remind you
that you come into life
with no indebtedness at all.
I know there are those
who have trudged through miserable lives
believing somehow
that they were paying back old debts.
Do you see how dishonest fear can be?
You come free because Love called you,
not because you owe somebody something.

What is karma? I will say this as softly as possible.

Karma is fear's excuse
for unhappiness.

**Where was the Light in this Angel's childhood?
It was miserable!**

The hurt child in each one of you
feels justified in being angry.
"Why would I not?" you say.
"My childhood caused me
a great deal of pain."

I do recognize, and so do you,
the incredible heaviness of anger.
Bitterness is the substance
with which the chains of your life are forged.
You all harbor
some of this quality of resentment,
wishing things had been different.
You cannot change them now,
nor is there any need,
for what you experienced then
is what has brought you
to this moment of revelation.
Let it be seen with gratitude.

Every child's dream
is that someday the parents will turn
and say, "You were right."
I can promise you
that when you leave your physical bodies,
the fact of having been right in your infancy
will be absolutely irrelevant.

When you reach the top of the mountain,
you will see all things clearly.
You will be astounded
at how many bouquets of roses
you will want to send to those
whom you now consider,
if not your outright enemies,
certainly not champions of your life.
A thank-you note to all tyrants will be most in order,
for they have brought you to the moment of Now.
Whatever brings you to your truth is a friend.

"Well," you may ask,
"couldn't I have reached the moment of Now
without them?" Evidently not
or you would have chosen another way.

Is abortion ever right?

There are no succinct answers to this
because each individual
is a soul incarnate.
You must walk your own way
to find your own answers
to the best of your ability at any given moment.
It is a complex world you live in, dear ones,
and it does not beg one single, simple answer.

Abortion offers those involved
an opportunity to probe the meaning
of their own self-love
and their own belief system
about life after death and life before birth.
Those indirectly involved stand peripherally
and make judgments.
For almost everyone
who has ever been confronted with that issue
it has been a useful time for self-exploration.

Do you believe
that an Angel does not know what to anticipate?
If the vehicle is not to come to term,
then there is no soul, no Angel,
to inhabit the body that is being formulated.
Now, how does one know
what the future decision will be?
In human terms that knowledge is impossible.
To the Greater Knowing
all things are preordained.

Abortion is one of the endless questions.
Each human being must decide individually.
There is a "yes" for one
and a "no" for another.
There will never be regulations
satisfactory to everyone.
Why? You did not come to be regulated.
You came as Angels within human bodies,
to live respectful of the human condition,
compassionate to the suffering of your world,
and at the same time to remember
that all things are eternally in the hands
of perfect Love.

The issue of abortion
has been one of the many useful teachers
on your planet today.
Some teachers are fading;
others are just rising
into the zenith of their effectiveness.
The nuclear threat to the world
was also a powerful professor for a long time.
It no longer has supreme attention-getting authority.
Other things are moving up.

Until the final soul has graduated,
there will always be a curriculum
upon your plane: abortion, AIDS,
small local skirmishes
that have enormous global effect,
nuclear power, the rights of people
to a home, food in their stomachs,
and clothes on their backs.
These are penetrating issues now.

As humanity moves
up the ladder of experience,
the teachings will become more complex,
more demanding, more compelling.
I am not in any way suggesting
that there will be monstrous earth changes
or terrible holocausts.
I am reminding you that on an individual basis,
the world offers endless opportunity for study.

What can we tell someone when they are in pain?

The first thing to tell them
is that they are loved,
not by some impersonal or invisible being,
but by you standing with them.
The doorway to any truth
is the one labeled "LOVE."

When that can be heard,
then the vaster reaches of Love can be believed.
When human addresses human,
there is a tendency to believe the person
rather than the philosophy.
That is quite appropriate,
because the suffering takes place
within the personal experience,
so it must be within that area
that one first reaches for solace.
If one could leap to broader understanding
and announce "I know I am an Angel,"
there would be no suffering,
just another point of interest on the journey.

The most important thing anyone can say
from an open heart
is "I am here and I love you."
This is not meant
to blanket someone else's experience,
but to be with them in their pain.

Human experience
is not some parasitic growth
upon the consciousness of the being.
It is the chosen journey.

When fear steps out, miracles can step in.
Will they always transform circumstances
as the compassionate friend would wish?
No.
Since everyone is embarked
upon their specific journey of love,
then all you can offer them is yourself.
You are the balm.
You are the sermon.
Perhaps the immediate benefit cannot be seen.
It is a call to faith.

Is humanity sinking into immorality?

To the contrary,
humanity is spiraling upward.
Things have been much more dank
and dark than this.
Today's capacity to communicate
is a wondrous device for truth,
although I know there is also great nonsense,
indeed harmful information,
disseminated through your media.
One's cells become permeated with terror
upon watching the usual fare of the television meal.
Yet it also holds a capacity to display
the shadowy sides of your human world.
Once people see what is happening,
they cannot pretend they do not know.

The majority of the planetary inhabitants
are evolving with the same rapidity as you are.
They see the same pain,
the same environmental outrage,
the same sad results of greed, of cruelty.
There are few who remain
stubbornly blind to all that.
The call of awakening comes
with every generation.
Immorality in governments
may turn your stomachs, but a century ago
it would not be known.
That alarm bell would not be sounded.

Fear will always find a way
to bring darkness, given the chance,
for that is the atmosphere of its survival.
The eruption of hostility
need not be seen as a step backward.
It is an emergence of the social abscesses
that were always there.
We are cleaning the sublayers.
The long-denied terrors
are being given public airing.

Is there anything we should do?

Rush to support the beneficial.
Speak out.
Do not let the ennui of fear
persuade you that you are powerless.
There is always something you can do
as long as you move
with the integrity of Love.

We are walking subtle lines here.
When one points to "negativity out there,"
it becomes judgment.
One cannot help but see, but one *can* help judging.
"Then what should I do with this?" you ask.
Open your heart that much wider
to an immoral leader. That does not mean you
support his actions.
"There is my teacher," you say.
"He is walking on a journey just as I am.
There goes an Angel
with a most demanding curriculum."

Can we really change things in our world?

*Everything you do
affects your entire planet.
Just one moment
of open-hearted allowing
and your planet is transformed.
All those who are breathing the atmosphere
inhale that much more Light.*

The world is changing rapidly,
for the journeys of many
are being completed in these times.
There are many souls
who will choose to return to spirit,
for there is indeed
the upward path of remembering.
There are also those who come
in willing service and walk
into the very depths of darkness
to help shake loose those

who, in their terror, would still cling
to what darkness seems to promise.
No soul is ever lost,
but forgetting can be profound,
can it not?

If you can stop one moment of inhumanity,
you must do so,
because you are part of the Plan as well,
but bring as much Love
to that moment as you can.

What is to be done?
Look for the Light smiling at you
through the apparent shadows,
and remember there is nothing
that transforms darkness more quickly
than a festivity right in the middle of it.
Today would be a perfect time to begin to celebrate
your angelhood.

Will you fall into forgetting again?
Of course, and you will awaken again.
Each time you remember,
the delight of your heart will explode
into a million twinkling stars.

Do not wait for perfection
to be the continuous way
in which you live
before you celebrate.
Whenever there is a crack
in the shell of illusion, give a party.
When you catch the sun
streaming through the clouds,
buy yourself a dozen roses.
Whenever you feel
like waltzing down the street,
let nothing stop you.

Is joy the dance? Is that all there is?

Yes.
To get to that joy,
one must recognize in oneself
and in others
that the suffering is not the person.
Joy is.
A miracle is waiting for you—
not to create it, but to remember it.

You are not a beggar at the table of life.
You are the honored guest.

7
Unlocking
the Door

To love yourselves is the final hurdle,
the definitive frontier of humanity.

Illusion delights
in embellishing its own importance.
"I must earn the right to enlightenment,"
you say, "by doing ten thousand prostrations,
by sitting for long periods of time
in great discomfort,
by fasting until I am almost dead,
by devoting at least seven lives
to the unselfish service of the poor.
Then perhaps..."

You recognize
the falsity of this and you rebel.
Then you scold yourselves for resisting.
"I'll never be enlightened," you lament,
"because I really don't *want* to live
on air and water."

Then someone whom you cannot even see
with physical eyes tells you, "No. No.
All you have to do is to fall in love
with yourselves and dare to trust
in your own profound goodness,
and along the way you should allow in every joy,
every celebration, every moment of delight.
You will find *that* to be the shortest distance
between your current illusion and Home."
I offer you this challenge.

Some of you fear
that when you die
there will be an awesome tribunal
sitting in judgment upon you.
The truth of the matter is
that the first thing you see
when you leave your bodies is Light,
the first thing you hear is laughter,
and the first thing you feel
is Love.

Fall in love with yourselves.
It is the next step upon your journey,
in fact it is the only remaining step.
Self-love demands
that you close forever the ledgers of your life
and that you move unencumbered
into the realization of your dreams
and your visions.

First you must revere yourselves
and from that enlightened viewpoint,
all circumstances in life
dance before you as opportunity.

There will never be anything new
said upon your planet.
There is no new message, no new key.
Indeed, there is no new viewpoint
and certainly there are no new promises.
The truth was given centuries ago
and has been repeated
ever since in different vocabularies
by different agents.

There comes a time in a human life
when what has been heard over and over,
suddenly, for some unknown reason,
stands before you
as undeniable and blessed reality.
So truth must be repeated
as often as there is someone to listen.

The moment you are fully present
in your self-love,
you will recognize wisdom
where it has always been.
In the meantime,
the spirits in your company
will continue their task of reminding you
until the moment comes when you
touch that memory within yourselves.

You did not choose to become human
to then escape your lives.
You came to live them,
and live them you will.
Some of you may choose
to remain distanced.
You have all felt the pain of such distancing
after moments of love,
of glory, when you feel alienated
from the feast of life, still hungry
and perhaps more empty than before
the feast began.
"Will I never be satisfied?" you wonder.
"Will I always seek another love, another God,
another healing, religion, path,
a new salvation?"

Never forget
that you carry your own laboratory
of salvation within you.

What are some other ways to help us remember?

Bring one question into each day:
"Where is Love here?"

Spend each day looking for Truth.
It will come in many forms:
a child's smile, the feel of rain on your hand,
the opening of a flower.
Keep vigilant.

Read the holy books of all religions.
You will find truth.
Distorted?
Of course, humanity wrote it down,
but it is there.

Practice meditation.
The world of fragmentation
cannot move to Oneness,
but Oneness can move
in the world of fragmentation
without departing from Itself.
Meditation becomes a means
by which you can sever your allegiance
with the active mind
and regain connection and devotion
to the *Self*.

Remind yourselves as often as possible
each day that you are Angels.

When you discover
that you have forgotten your angelhood,
let that be a moment of rejoicing.
Your noticing transforms the illusion again.
For that instant you are free.

Is there some way for mind to be an ally?

The mind, in its fundamental nature, *is* an ally.
Mind is simply the cap you have chosen to wear
and it will serve whatever intention
you consciously make.
It is most willing to join the heart,
but first you must be willing to disengage
from your contract with fear.

You cannot walk mindless.
Not only would you bump into things,
you would fail the purpose
for which you have come.
Mind has untapped capacities
to remind you of the gift of wonder
that *You* are,
once you have instructed it to do so.
But your instructions must come from Love,
or they will, no matter
how sweetly they are worded,
turn against the truth.

Mind, having been skillfully designed,
finds itself a thing of pride.
"Am I not excellent and many times clear?"

Yes, mind,
you are, and you are essential
to the journey of the human being
and by extension for the journey of the Angel.
The Angel cannot shrink itself to mind's size,
but can utilize the mind,
saying, "Mind is a fine tool,
and it is truly becoming to the human costume.
Even though I am much more than mind,
I can employ it in my service."
Your decision to choose Love
automatically invites mind's support.

**What can we look for to help us
fall in love with ourselves?**

As long as you are not present in your lives
here and now, you will indeed continue to search
for some holy grail outside of the *Self*.
You will never find it.

There is no greater wisdom
than your own heart.
That can be a disturbing thought
if you have lost faith in your heart.
It can seem like a pronouncement
that if you cannot yet remember
that you are an Angel,
you will be forever entombed
in human dissatisfaction.

I would encourage you all
to hold what I say as absolute truth.
Love is the only reality.
All the rest is just so much traffic noise.
You all come together from time to time
to remind each other of that,
to remember that you are safe,
that you are on a holy journey,
and that what you hope is true is,
in fact, the truth.
Self-love is your passage through.

I suggest that you look
past your imagined historic defects.
There is gravity pulling you down, dear ones,
why would you not stumble from time to time?
Consider this...you come from angelhood,
so you are not used to standing
upon very heavy feet.

If you rely on the outer world
to verify your existence,
you will never find yourselves,
for you are looking through your own
warped concepts into distorted mirrors.
Ask yourselves these questions:
"Do I love myself
when someone is shouting angrily at me?
Do I love myself
when I have disappointed others?
Do I love myself
when I feel I have failed?
What makes me stop loving myself?"

Let me remind you,
Love is not something to be earned.
It cannot be judged,
meted out, or taken away.
Love is something that you *are*.

In the miracle of the perfect Love that *You* are,
there is no duality. There is no "other."
There is only *You* and your compassion,
your Divine intent.
Such a Love cannot be understood by the mind,
because mind lives within the world of illusion.
You do not.

Without your loving presence, the
Divine Plan is incomplete.

Do not hover on the threshold
to look around with fear-filled eyes.
You cannot bargain.
You cannot hope for any guarantee.
You can only unlock the door
that keeps you imprisoned and leap into Love.

How does one unlock the door
to one's habitual premise of reality?
Begin with this:

Let your imagination
conjure up the locked door.
It can take any design you prefer,
any color or shape.

Sit for a moment with the intent
to go beyond that door.

How do you approach this door?
Running? Walking? On tiptoe?
What are you feeling?

How will you open it?

Will you use a key? An ax?
Do you call a locksmith?
A blacksmith?
Will you just knock?

Become aware of how you
go about unlocking the imaginary door.
It will be revealing.

If you can find wherein your "no" is present,
then the "yes" can be freed.
That will fling open the door
to wondrous adventure.

**Is the best way to experience the Angel in us
to be content with the human?**

Absolutely.
There is no contentment in avoidance of life.
To say yes to life does not mean that you
laud the painful or embrace the darkness.
Your yes brings *You*, the Being of Light,
into the center of you, the human.
When the Light
is brought into the darkened room,
there is no room for darkness.

The moment you die (and each one of you
will come to that happy circumstance in time)
you want to dance.
"Wasn't that wonderful!" you say.
"Poignant? Yes.
Painful? I don't remember,
but I can imagine the disappointments
I must have felt. The entire thing
was a moment of perfection. Every bit."

**Two people I know, one as a result of trauma
and the other while just crawling under a fence,
each reported a period of time
when they saw everything around them
as particles of light—
grass, bodies, trees, stones, everything danced
as moving light. What was that?**

They experienced a journey out of the familiar
into the real.
And what really *is* is dancing Light.

When we remember who we are,
will our lives suddenly change?

Yes and no.
Outer circumstance, made of denser stuff,
requires more time to shift direction,
but inner experience
of that same circumstance
can alter immediately and never return
to what it was before.

Yet, this becomes subtle.
As Beings of Light who have chosen again
to come into human form,
your task is to honor the voice that called you.
That voice was not fear.
It was Love.
So to allow things to *be* is, perhaps,
the greatest act of faith
that human beings can offer themselves.
One does not have to look far
to touch a place of anguish
or disappointment or suffering
in your personal or global world.
It demands a leap of faith to bear witness
to such things and not rush to change them.

Emmanuel, can Earth help us to remember Home?

The similarities are distorted.
Anything that is physically manifested
cannot fully and completely
represent the consciousness that created it,
because the very act of physical manifestation
freezes something into shape and form,
whereas the reality of consciousness
is ever-changing.

The palette of human understanding
is so much less rich than the colors that truly exist.
Perhaps this exercise will give you a hint:

What do you want heaven to be like?
Do not be modest or reasonable.

What do you want your present life to be like?
Do not be sensible.
Allow no limitations at all.
The colors of the universe cannot
be contained in sensible proportion.

**How do vibrant color and soft texture
translate on your plane?**

You all find it comfortable and necessary
to trust the sensing devices of your bodies.
If you did not have feelings in your fingers,
would you know texture?
Would you know color
without your ocular equipment?

As you see color, you perceive its energetic quality
and the eyes report "I see blue."
But that is the translation.
What you are truly experiencing
is an energetic effect upon the retina of the eye.

Do you find a colorless realm here at Home?
Indeed you do not.
You come to colors that sing
without the necessity for pigmentation.
You find textures
without the need for solid manifestation.
There is not much more I can tell you,
because there is no vocabulary available
between us to convey what I experience.
The nearest thing might be the feel
of a warm breeze upon your body.
A breeze refuses to be frozen.
Or perhaps the song of a bird.
You receive the notes fleetingly,
but before they can be given substance,
they are gone.

Well, how does Earth compare to Home?

Your world is a world of symbols,
a world of labels,
a world of hope made manifest.
Look at yourselves.
Do your physical bodies represent the Angel?
Perhaps in moments of great Love.
Certainly just before you were born
there was the vibrancy of spirit entering into form.
Shortly after birth, however,
you begin to say, "This is who I am."
In that statement,
you congeal yourselves into illusion.
Language is no friend to greater truth,
for the understanding of words—
semantics itself—is part of the freezing process.

I promise you, when you begin to truly see,
you will greet Angels everywhere,
and this will remind you of Home.
You will note with compassion
the pain and the struggle,
the nobility of purpose,
the golden intent of the human being.
That same golden intent, that nobility,
is much like Home as well.

Is there a world in spirit which is round
and beautiful, spinning through the universe?
There is no need.
You have created your world.
You have also created all the stars
in your heavens to honor the process
with which you are now so deeply engaged.
When the final soul awakens,
what will happen to your planet
and all the creatures upon it?
They will all come Home,
but not in the shapes
in which you now perceive them.
Physically manifested form is not worn
where you come from.

Trust that every human Angel
is just as homesick as you are.
No matter how dark your world may seem now,
no matter how riddled with terror,
immorality, dishonesty, thievery,
murder, and unthinkable crime of all sorts,
every human being is destined to awaken.
Ultimately the entire human race
will remember its unity.
Meanwhile, you will return to the planet
time and time again until that final soul
has touched the darkness with Light.
Is that to be soon?
Not so soon that you will applaud it
in the physical bodies
you are currently wearing.

**How can we practice expansion
into a larger dimension of reality?**

Begin to allow moments of spontaneity
their full flower. Close your eyes
and imagine:

*You are given a passport and means of travel
through all the other realms and dimensions
that you might possibly dream exist.*

How would you want it all to be?

What sort of beings would you like to meet?

What experiences would you like to have?

What questions would you ask?

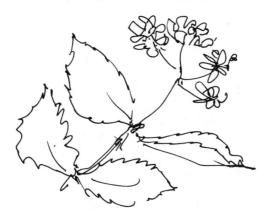

**If we incarnate to do certain work
and also have free choice,
can you talk about the dance between action and control,
take-charge and let-go?**

Must you be consciously surrendered
to the will of the soul?
It might make it easier for you,
but that does not mean
that if you are not surrendered
you will not accomplish the purpose
for which you come.
You come to do specific things,
but there is no demand that they be done
in specific ways.
The soul leaves to the human personality
the inventive wanderings into illusion.

To bring Light into the darkness,
you must go there yourself.
The human being may seem to stumble and fall,
but the soul is doing its work.
There is no perfect balance
between surrender and striving.
There is no way you can derail the train
upon which you ride.
You can choose a more comfortable coach,
perhaps, but the train
is bound to reach its destination.

"Then why do I bother with all this striving?"
you might ask yourselves.

Because that is who you are.
You will wander in unknowing,
and at the very nadir of failure,
when you blame yourself the most,
if you can remember your angelhood,
you will have the joy of realizing that you have,
in fact, succeeded.
In whatever manner the human personality
experiences a life, the soul will do its work.
So it is the human personality
that faces the moment of choice.
The soul has already made its selection.

You cannot fail.
How do you wish to travel the way?
Would you like to dance it?
Crawl it? Enjoy? Suffer? Laugh or weep?
Do you want to remain in the grasp of illusion
or turn to the heart and let it lead
you out to Light?
Whatever mode you choose,
you must know that there is nothing
that can stop you.

A soul is too vast a perfect wisdom
to lose its way.

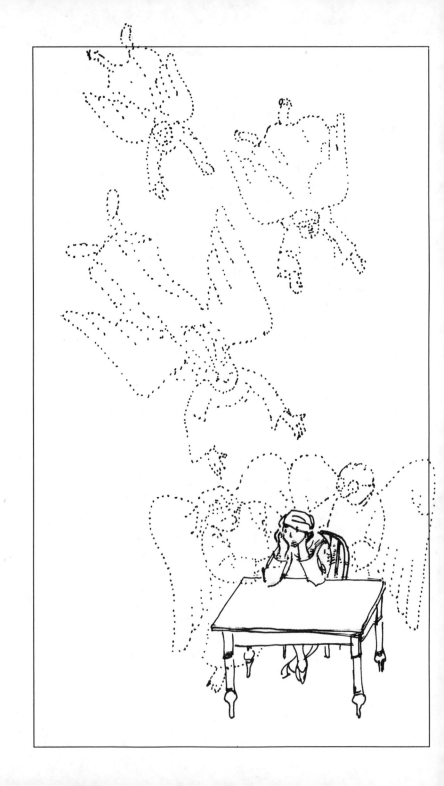

8
Angelic Conceptions and Misconceptions

An Angel will appear
in whatever manner
you need to see it.

When I was a little girl,
my mother told me that I had a guardian Angel
watching over me.
Is there an Angel that is particularly for me?

There is indeed
an Angel that is absolutely
and particularly for you.
Each person has one of those dear Beings,
perhaps several.
In various moments of crisis
or of vast importance in your life,
when the turning point
must be met in the name of the soul's intent,
there is more than one Angel
gathered around you.

Yes, you walk with an Angel.
That is a comfort to a child.
To the mature adult I would say,
"You never left the Oneness."
There are not only many Angels with you,
but eternity is with you.
You are wrapped in perfect Love.
One cannot be so vast
in speaking to a small child.
The child is asking one thing.
"Is there any other being
who is with me like the me I still remember?"
The child really wants to know,
"Is the truth of me still alive?"
The answer is yes.

There is, however, an even greater reality.
Eternal Love, the perfection of All-That-Is,
is alive and waiting within you.
The boundaries that seem to separate you
from your guardian Angel
are the boundaries of illusion.

Oneness abides completely
and uninterrupted
within the world of separation.
It is only that the eyes are taught
to see difference and "otherness"
rather than to soften to perceive the One.

**Emmanuel, why can't we see you
and the other Angels we know are there?**

That is not a deliberate deprivation,
but a requirement for entering
into the world of fabricated reality.
You all have moments
when you see the Light clearly,
when you touch a form
that has no physical endowments.
At such times, your heart leaps with joy
and then in the next moment you wonder
if you should get your glasses checked.

**Sometimes I seem to hear my name called
when I am in meditation. Is that an Angel?**

Who calls your name?
I do, in one of the myriad forms
in which I touch your world.

How can we learn to call upon these Beings
that we cannot see as we go about our daily lives?
Can you tell us some ways
to have more of a sense of their presence
or to have a conversation with them?

Remember that you, the human being,
are also the Angel that is your essence.
If you can align yourself with that truth,
then your connection with all Angels
is open and flowing.
If you believe you are reaching out
from an inner unworthiness,
desperation, or endangerment
to find some help,
it is much more difficult for us to reach you.
We walk with you.
We speak with you.
We teach you.
We caress you and comfort that portion of you
that is in physical form until such a time
as the remembering begins to take hold.
Then, more and more, your vision clears
and you walk both in the world of spirit
and the world of physically materialized matter
with equal awareness.

Surrounding your planet
is absolute and eternal perfection.
That is who *You* are.
That is our Home. Walk with us.
We belong together.

How to call upon your accompanying Angel?
I would suggest that when you are joyful,
when you feel no need to be rescued,
that is a good time to touch those Beings
who cannot be seen by the physical eye.
Ask, "Are you there now
when I am watching the beautiful sunset?
When I am holding the hand of someone I love?
When I am listening to my favorite music?
Are you there in my peace
and in my centeredness?"

There are many ways
to communicate with your Angel.

Let the mind become quiet
so that the chatter of human life is muffled.
Then the deeper knowing can be perceived.
Sit with pen and paper and just allow yourself
to begin to write. Write what?
Begin by writing what you want the Angel to say to you.

Is that fabrication?
It may appear contrived, but it is a beginning.

If you were to be addressed by the Angel
who walks with you, what would you want it to say?
How would you want it to begin contact with you?
Then imagine it just that way.
What kind of a love letter
do you want your guardian Angel to write you?
Just begin.

There will be severe doubts. Release them.
Mind will give you dire warnings. Ignore them.
Offer yourselves the pleasure of beginning
to create the letter you have always wanted
to receive. There will come a moment
when *you* are not writing the letter.
The letter will be writing itself. Trust.
You will have begun your communication.

The doorway is always open
from our side to yours.
It is seldom open from your side to ours
until you have determined for yourselves
that the most important object
of human experience is to know the God *Self*.
Then it becomes remarkably easy
to look around and see nothing but Angels,
to hear nothing but heavenly music.

There are many more people who see Angels
walking upon the planet
than you are given to know. Why?
Well, if you were to go to your office
and say "I just spoke with Angels
and I heard heavenly music,"
you might be held suspect, might you not?
The truth of angelic beings,
although it is making headway,
has still a great way to go to dissuade
the doubting mind that doubt is reasonable.

At night, before I drift off to sleep,
I visually perceive the outlines of a luminous presence.
My limited self panics a bit and it's hard
to remain in that presence very long.
Can you advise me as to how to understand
this experience so it doesn't frighten me
and I can work with it skillfully?

Whenever a luminous presence
enters into your life,
know that Grace has taken form.

How to work with it?
Well, when one asks a question in that way,
one wonders what "work"
could possibly be accomplished?
I suggest that you open your heart
and enjoy its company.

Why do you assume
that something needs to be done?
There is no danger in the unknown.
There is certainly no menace in a Being of Light
who loves you and blesses you,
who has been with you through eternity
and has come to remind you, "I am here."

Is there such a thing as a dark Angel?

No, there is not.
Of course, Angels can appear
in whatever guise suits their purpose.
Our costuming is quite deliberate.
For instance,
there can be absolutely impish Angels
who delight the heart of the lonely
and suppressed child.
Psychology might decide
that the "imaginary" companion—
playful and bold, courageous and jolly—
was simply the part of that child
that dared not show itself.
We will reach you any way we can,
not because you are lost,
but because that is what we promised you.

Before you were born
you said to us, "Remember, don't let me get lost.
Be there with me all the time,
tapping me on the shoulder to remind me,
because I know I will forget."

We have done exactly that.
We have called you from treetops.
We have whispered through the breeze.
We have touched your hands in times of terror
or loneliness.
We have embraced you in your pain.
We have laughed with your joy.
Did you know that? Somewhere, yes.

But are there forces that would like us not to remember?

Fear.
That is about as forceful as illusion can get.
Yet not one of you is a victim of fear.
Fear is a choice, an automatic response.
It is an addiction, a rabbit's foot
you believe will keep you safe.
You think if you are afraid,
then you will be always alert and aware
and beyond all danger.

Is fear a force beyond the self?
No, but fear itself can seem to expand
as though it were a giant.
Humanity has placed at fear's doorstep
many symbols, the devil being one.
There is no darkness outside your own belief.
How can the Light be lost?

Darkness lives only within the world of illusion.
Will science discover that?
To a great extent it already has.
Scientists will soon report,

*"At the end of our most powerful instruments
of perception, all we see is Light."*

Can you tell me about some of the forms
that Angels have taken when people try to picture them?
For example, they are often painted with beautiful wings.

You are asking me to talk about symbols.
All-That-Is, where Angels exist,
has no need to conform to form.
Such personification of Love is memory
seeking to break through the shroud of forgetting
and say, "Don't you see?
I'm not a painting on the wall. I'm a mirror!"

The heart can represent angelhood
only in accordance
with available symbolic vocabulary.
What do wings denote?
They suggest flight, beauty, freedom.
These are excellent images, so when Angels
come to you, if you want them to have wings,
you will see wings.
Do they need physical wings to move outside
your planetary atmosphere? Of course not.

Love can be anywhere It likes
and can create anything It wishes.
How does one symbolize that?
As wings—the essence of wings
without the baggage.

The image of Angels
sitting upon clouds, playing harps,
was comforting for a long time to many people.
For some it still is.
The idea of spirit guides
clothed in various ethnic costumes
and personalities is also reassuring.
"All right," we in spirit say, "it doesn't matter.
Whatever allows the remembering,
we comply gladly."
Perhaps even God, for a time,
must be some distant and arbitrarily
judgmental figure sitting on a throne
and hurling down thunderbolts.
Well, if that gives people a sense of safety
(and oddly enough, it does), then let it be so.

Am I the same sort of Angel as the Angel Gabriel?

Almost to a T.

**There are some teachings that suggest
that there is a parallel evolution between
the angelic kingdom and the human kingdom.
Is that accurate, and, if so, how does that fit
with the Angel within ourselves
in the human kingdom?**

Parallel evolution is not part of my experience
or what I teach.
There is a belief that the world of spirit
somehow must function
as the human world does.

Creation does not require evolution.
Its nature is constant unfoldment.

*You are an Angel
as well as a struggling human,
but you are not
a struggling Angel.*

**In the Bible they talk about Seraphim and Cherubim and hierarchies of Angels.
Is that inaccurate?**

The world must embellish what it cannot know
with a panoply of understandable symbols
or it becomes confused.
All the illusion that has given rise
to such available, understandable beings
does so to people the vast and screaming void
of its own loneliness.
The mind would not rest peacefully
if the response to all its longing and fear
was to say "Somewhere within that fear
is a point of Light. Go find it."

Is God a sentient being?

When *You* are walking around in human form,
You are.

Is sex sometimes a way to find the angelic?
In the writings about Angels,
there is concern about their gender.
Also, do we keep our maleness or our femaleness as Angels?

The vehicle of sexual expression
is often clouded by the enormous amount
of illusion you carry into moments of intimacy.
The human race is taught first to hide its angelhood
and then in moments of sexual union,
when the heart is longing to touch Oneness
through the body, fear steps in and threatens,
"You'd better not be discovered here!"
Seldom, then, is sexuality ever a means
by which Divine union is touched,
although it certainly holds that capability.

The moment of childbirth, as well,
could be the sun bursting through the clouds
of remembering if one were allowed to give birth
in the confidence that it was the choice
of three souls—mother, father, child—
and that having a child
is the ultimate act of creation for a human being.
It need not be paid for by disharmony, pain,
and postpartum depression.
There is nothing on your human planet
that if allowed its full nature
will not reflect the light of God.
There is nothing on your planet that
when viewed without the lenses of opinion
and judgment (which are historic
in each one of you) will not stand before you
as perfect Love. Nothing.

As long as you wear a physical body,
gender is absolutely essential.
When you are not wearing one, it is no longer needed.
The gender necessity comes
because you are encased
in a seemingly solid physical form,
and sexuality is a practical means
by which you can reach one to another,
a vehicle of Love, a means by which hearts
can touch through the density of human form.
Once you are denuded of your physical bodies,
you become one with all things.
Is that not what sexual union is seeking, Oneness?
If there is no barrier to Oneness,
there is no need for a vehicle to overcome it.

Do not mourn the fact
that you will leave behind the pleasures of sexuality
when you come Home.
They are but dim representatives
of the awaiting bliss.

How do we relate to Angels?

With a great deal of joy.
There comes a time on the path up the mountain
when one begins to meet Angels
more and more frequently.
They start out by seeming to be
just ordinary people, then suddenly
one realizes that these ordinary people
are quite extraordinary.
When you become acquainted
with their extraordinary qualities,
you begin to perceive that these qualities
hold a great deal of spirit.

As you continue up the mountain
you find human beings who seem to be more spirit
than human and then you begin to notice
that there are spirits who make only the most
cursory effort at being human.
Perhaps they are all members of SOAR
(Society of Angels Remembering).

9
Tumultuous Homecomings out of This World

Death is a release into the joy of Homecoming.

You are born into a world that insists upon death.
From the human point of view, death is a defeat.
Death is not your enemy. It is your ticket Home.
Dying is not failure.
It is the means by which you can rid yourself
of the physical body.
You die into no danger, no illness, no falsity,
no betrayal, no guesswork. *You* remain.

What lives, then?
Your profound, illuminated, loving truth.

Do not let your imagination
paint death through the mind's palette.

Regardless of how it may seem
in the physical world, from my point of view
death is a gentle leave-taking
and a joyous Homecoming.
As a human being dies, there is always someone,
somewhere, who travels from sleep
to be with that person until he or she is lifted
enough to touch the hands of the Angels,
lest lingering habits of viewpoint
make a moment of confusion.
The call goes out: Who will come?
Who could better fill that service than one
who is still human and whose sleeping body
allows the freedom to answer?

You are greeted at death by all those beings
with whom you have lived and loved,
not only in the life you just left,
but in each life you have ever had.
Of course, those beloveds who
had already reincarnated onto planet Earth
have just bid you good-bye at your exit.

**When we get back to God, will we be conscious
of the people we once were?**

Not only conscious,
but I want to tell you something delightful.
After every lifetime, at the gathering
of those with whom you have shared that life,
there is a wonderful exchange.
Great clarity comes from that.
Since you are all free from fear and illusion,
you enjoy it enormously.

**How do I deal with the pain of not having
the physical presence when a loved one dies?**

Grieve for the loss of the physical embodiment
of a Love you have always known,
and mourn it to the depths of your human despair,
but do not believe it. The loss is temporary.

When a physical body dies, as it must,
you find yourselves missing the human presence.
Of course. The touch, the voice, the smell
of another human being with whom
you have walked in Love; these things are very dear.
Since the Love you feel is eternal,
in that sense there is no loss,
but you bear reverence to the packaging.
Love cannot remain with you in that form.
If you allow the essence of that Love,
you can touch it still, regardless of where
the physical body is.

It is the essence of Love
that calls forth the physical.
It is never the other way around.
That love is eternally with you,
whether it manifests in physical form or not.
Though your missing is real, the eternal promise
is more so, for once Love has joined together,
it remains always.

Will you see your beloved again?
Of course you will.
Perhaps the meeting will take place
during this life in another body,
or when you yourself return Home,
or the next time you join hands and joyously
leap together into a form.

Be absolutely present in grief
and sorrow will turn to something else—
loving memory, a thank-you,
something healing and sweet.
Must you feel pain in loving?
When you are human, perhaps yes,
until you are willing to know Love
beyond the arena of physicality.

Allow the costume to be changed.

**When those who have died take rebirth,
do we find them again?**

Loved ones come together time and time again.
How could you look at anyone
and pretend to see a stranger?
How could you love anyone and not know
that you have loved them before?
How could it be that you would not know those
with whom you have walked
since you are all fabric of the One?

There have been flashes of recall
when one might say, "I know who you are.
You were my mother last time."
Well, yes, and perhaps the time before that
the soul may have existed in another area
of the universe. You have all known each other
before because you *are* each other.

Your companions in a human life hold promises
with you. One might almost say
that you sign a contract in the world of spirit,
although that seems depressingly businesslike.
Your contract states "I will be with you
because I am part of you, because I love you."

Then you come to Earth
and you find each other, either through birth
or what seems to be the accidents
of adult meeting. The time comes
when one of you leaves and the other, bereft,
continues to live his or her life.
The one who has died might want
to quickly turn around and come back.
When you leave your physical body,
you recognize the total truth
of the entire venture, and some of you
are so enthusiastic that you say,
"I'd like to go back immediately."

We who await you at this side of death caution,
"Don't you think you might want to rest a little?"
"No. No. No," you insist, "I have it now.
I'm going right back again before I forget."

Of course, until you are actually born,
you do indeed "have it."
Then you are thrust into the world of illusion again.
But Love never forgets Itself.
If those you have loved are alive on the planet,
you will seek them out in all manner
of seemingly impossible circumstances.

*You never forget the beings you have loved,
and they never forget you.*

**Two friends were suddenly killed in a car crash.
Are they all right?**

Of course they are.
Death is not traumatic to the dying.
One moment you are alive and then you are not,
and there is little difference except you are free.

Do not anguish over what seems to be
the circumstances of sudden and chaotic death.
In truth, there is no such thing as "chaotic" anything,
and death itself is always most pleasant
to those who have died.
As spirits swiftly join them, the newly dead realize
that they have just graduated from school.

The image of a dead human being in a box
being lowered into the earth (that strikes terror
in everybody's heart) exists only in the paper world
of human experience.
By the time the burial takes place,
the inhabitant of the box has long since departed—
although he may briefly attend his own funeral.

Fear has told you that you will not have enough time
to complete whatever you have come to do.
Fear is wrong.

No physical body dies
one moment before the soul is ready,
nor one moment after.

You will satisfy the call of Love
that brought you here no matter what circumstances
your human personality presents,
no matter what hurdles must be surmounted
within your life or your world.
You will return Home fulfilled.
That may seem a strange thing to say
when faced with "untimely" death,
but it is the mind's clock
that proclaims it untimely, not the soul's.

You cannot imagine how many times
the swinging door of death has opened to receive you
and opened again to allow you to take birth.
The moment you are born,
you are anticipating the exit sign.

Tell a dying loved one
that the celebration is already arranged.
All the beings ever loved will be there at the greeting.
That is not some simplistic description,
but a limited way of saying "All is well."
Fear is left at the deathbed.
If one is willing, it can be left now
by breathing a soft "yes"
into the fact of death itself.

**My father died last month.
Can I help him on his journey?**

The human heart is the tenderest of instruments.
There is a profound and eternal sweetness
in every one of you.
If you would only remember it, honor it,
and live it, your world would move spontaneously
to be a most blessed place.

You miss the living form you called "father"
which is no longer here to remind you of the Love
that is in your heart. Your father has no need of help.
When you say "on his journey,"
you are viewing the process of dying
as a voyage in time and space.

Time and space end at the moment of death.
There is no journey. There is only yes.
There is only *Isness*. There is only perfect Love
and the expanded celebration of the man
who was your father into the glowing Angel.
Is that description symbolic?
Yes, and very close to accurate.

**How do those we love who have died
see us down here on Earth?
Do they see our every move, hear our every thought?**

Oh, dear, no.
It isn't that they are not interested in your welfare,
but they have been through that thought business
and they would rather receive you in another way.

How do they see you?
Why, they see you with the Love
that brought them to you to begin with.
They see your perfection. They see your courage.
They see your good intent and your devotion.
Even beneath the personality's disappointments
and outrages and vendettas,
they know who you really are.

If you are concerned
that your unlovingness toward them
and perhaps theirs toward you leaves a scar,
it does not. Are you forgiven everything?
It goes beyond that.
You will see the next time you die.
There is no need for forgiveness because the clarity
that is yours again once you leave your physical body
recognizes that nothing wrong has ever been done.

*No misunderstanding
lives through the dying process.*

**My four-year-old passed away from cancer.
I am at a peaceful place with her life and death
after fifteen years. Can I communicate with her now?**

The death of a child, the departure of a Love...
fifteen years is like one breath.
When one moves into such loss, one touches eternity.
To grief, eternity seems like every minute
since the child has been gone.
To Love, it seems but the briefest instant.
Not only will you see her again,
but you have never been without her.

When a child is born, the heavens open,
and life, truth, perfect Love flood in.
When a child dies,
it seems as though there has been a cruel hoax.
If someone of advanced age dies
you can say, "Well, they did what they came to do.
They lived a reasonable life span and now
they are going Home to rest."

The four-year-old scarcely seems
to have had the opportunity for a life at all.
What is meant by the early and abrupt leaving
of an Angel? Was there a mistake?
No, there was not.
Were there gifts to bring?
You know there were.
Were there things to be experienced
by the soul itself?
Yes, indeed, but never of a punitive nature.
None of you comes to learn punishing lessons.

Where is she now? Is she available for your contact?
Yes, she is, but she will become much more available
if you release the image of a small child
and allow in its place the immensity, the glory,
and the brilliance of the Love
that came and took the form of a small child.

If Love can come
and squeeze Itself into such a small form
and walk with you for a little while,
why does it not stay?
That question can be pondered only breath by breath
for the rest of this human incarnation.

Please remember that Love comes when called
and then Love takes form.
It is not form that elicits Love.
I promise, dear one, and so does she,
that at the moment of your departure
there will be a recognizable reunion.

How will you recognize her?
When she was alive,
you did not know her through her child's body.
You knew her through your Love,
which you equated with the physical presence.
You will know her, as we in spirit know you,
from the essence of who *She* is,
not from her costume,
certainly not from your labeled relationship,
and very little from the human experience.

Physicality is always secondary
in the recognition of Love.

Do we all have our own individuality through eternity?
Does love between two people continue?

You cannot love completely
while you are walking in human form
because the very nature of humanness
is predicated upon separation.
As your awareness expands,
it does not cling so fiercely
to the uniqueness of the individual personality.

When you move to remembering,
you know yourselves not just as human beings
and not just as members of your human families,
but you become a part of the community,
and of the nation, and then of the world.
From there you once again know yourselves
as the universe.

What does that do to interpersonal relationships
upon the Earth plane?
Does it mean that you become so vast
that you are depersonalized?
No. You expand to reclaim your capacity
to know all things.
What was once a simple familial love
becomes magnified a thousandfold.

When someone dies,
feel free to continue the conversation,
but know that you are not speaking
to the limited person that you knew.
You are speaking to the essence.

What about the choice to take one's own life
when one is dying in great pain?
Would you talk about that from the perspective
of our angelic nature? Is it ever justified?

It is always justified.
If someone does not wish to remain
and suffer intractable pain, why should they?

You might say,
"But my soul has chosen to come to this pain."
Then has not your soul also chosen
to become the human being
who would say, "I don't want to have this anymore"?

The mind holds such rigid definitions
of what is truth and what is falsehood,
what is soul and what is body,
what is life and what is death.
You do not die to move away from life but toward it.

There are many who will go to the end
of their physical body's natural capacity to endure.
That is their choice.
It must be honored, but not more highly
than the choice of those who decide that they
have had enough.

What is it like after death?

You might enjoy considering
what kind of an experience you would like it to be.
Think of it this way:

You can have anything you want.
What would you like to do?
You can do it.

What would you like to hear?
You will hear it.

What would you like to know?
You can know anything.

Who would you like to greet you?
Even if part of them has reincarnated,
the essence of their love
will be there for you.

(Those of you who just wanted to meet
your favorite grandmother may find when you die
that her energy is the same as that of your grandson
back on planet Earth.)

What is the best way
to help the dying leave their bodies?

Those of you who are called to such tender work
must first walk your own death,
not that you must physically leave your bodies
(you would be useful, but not nearly as effective
as you are *in* your bodies at this point).
You need to explore your own fears
of what dying means to you.
Those who are getting ready to die
are moving back to the sensitivity of the small child.
They are releasing the earthly illusion
and they are touching more wisdom
than they ever believed possible.
They are traveling back to the locked door
of the sanctuary within, and as they open that door,
they say, "Now, let us see who I really am."

If you fear death,
do not go near someone who is dying
unless you can tell him, "I am here in fear.
Will you be my teacher
by sharing your experience of dying?"
At that moment, of course, his heart will open
and he will answer, "Come on in,
the water isn't really bad at all."

To help someone die in peace, remind yourself—
and him—that he is going Home,
that he is leaving illusion and moving back into truth.
You have all experienced dreams that you knew
were not the usual sleeping dreams.
You have gone somewhere wonderful,
soft, loving, joyful, and lighted.
Believe those dreams. Encourage your dying friend
to believe in his own dreams.
They are visits Home.

When you know who *You* are,
you will instantly recognize that death
has nothing to do with you, but until that time,
you will hold opinions about it
as you hold opinions about life.
Make friends with death.

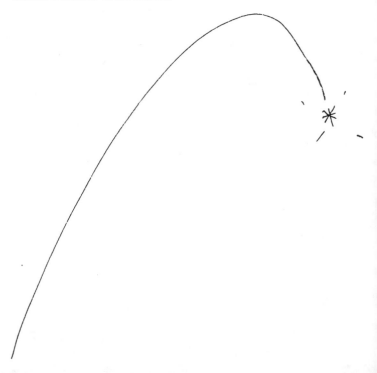

Dying can be the most exquisite experience
of a lifetime.
All the memories in all your accumulated lives
now accompany you because you are moving
to Oneness and bringing with you
everything of value that you have touched
and experienced and gathered.

All Love returns with you.
All fear returns to dust.

10
Time and Lives Past

Curiosity will lead you to eternity.

What can you tell us about time, Emmanuel?

From within time or from outside of time?

How about from outside of time?

Then there is no manner in which I can relate
to time at all.

I challenge you all to go beyond
even your imagined capacity to live
within a world that does not honor
clock and calendar.
You wonder how you might live
without the metronome of regulation.
Within the human world you could not,
for if time were eliminated,
a different device would swiftly be found
to avoid the fear of bumping one aspect
of one's busy day into another.

We could say that time is a master of restraint
devised by those who fear that chaos will erupt
if control is not maintained.
Beyond that, there is little more to be said.
You yourselves know in your busy lives
that time takes many different forms.
At one moment it is lengthy.
At another it seems that the powers-that-be
shrink a day of busyness into a smallness
too tight to encompass all your activities.

Time at best is only a device to be perceived
as a means of recognition,
a means of communication between
the world of demand and the world of inner self,
a way by which a filing system can
ostensibly be organized so that the dread
of too much involvement (or too little)
can be abated.

It is one of the greatest reliefs,
when you leave your physical bodies,
to recognize that you no longer
have to wear a watch.

A simple exercise might be useful here.

Take a moment to look at a watch.
Listen to its ticking, or notice its second hand.

Recognize how quickly one's very breath
becomes monitored and controlled by the ticking
of that mechanism
that holds no spiritual context
and was devised by no great authority.
It is simply a construction wherein a disk can connect
with another piece of the mechanism to turn hands
around an arbitrary face.

To go beyond the automatic response of bowing
to the clock and to welcome the more fluid aspects
of your relationship to time
will not render you ineffectual or unable to walk
within the timed world.

It will offer spaciousness
so that one is not screaming to squeeze oneself
within the domain of the tick-tock of time,
but can stand outside and, with authority,
utilize time where it can be fruitful.

You strive so valiantly to create a happy future.
You hold with such reverence the joy
as well as the pain of the past.
In so doing you rob yourselves
of the lives you have come to live,
for if you are living in history or anticipation,
you are not living in the moment.

It is not escape from time you seek. It is Love.
The longing for transformation is the soul's voice.
When you insist on understanding,
you remove yourselves from the moments of magic.
The power of such a moment is available to you
anytime you care to remember.
However, it requires that you do not label it
or demand of it anything except what is present
in the space of that breath.
If you can allow each moment its own uniqueness,
you will find a way through the forest.

Fear would welcome a lifetime answer
to all your questions.
It would prefer everything neatly wrapped
in understanding, yet that same packaging
would keep you from the moment
and you would sink again into the morass of illusion.
Recognize that there is no future and no past.
Each moment is filled with its own riches.
You live NOW.

**In therapy, shouldn't we go back in time
to explore our childhood?**

Whatever illusion you carry is occurring
every minute of your life until it is perceived.
If it is comforting to see it
in its historic moment of inception,
then do so, but do not linger in history.
Bring your findings to this moment,
for I promise you, every unhealed wound
you have ever borne is with you now.

"All I want is truth," you say.

When you discover the answer,
"Truth is who you are in this moment,"
mind demurs.
"Really, I don't think that's the truth I mean.
I had in mind something vaster than I am,
something a little more...well, reliable."

Your answer cannot be truth written in stone.
Truth dies when it is solidified.
It awaits you in the liquid sanctuary
of your own hearts.

**Is it possible to live more than one human life
simultaneously?**

Remove the illusion of time and space
and you have all things transpiring simultaneously
within the same instant of eternity.
The mind sees nothing but jumble and chaos in that.

One wonders, "Well, if I am me here, who else am I?
Where am I? What am I doing? What am I feeling?
Do I know about me?
Or is this 'me' completely forgotten
by the other me's?"

Within the illusion, you fragment at birth.
You must become many things
if you are to submerge yourselves in the clatter
of worldly contradictions.
In that fragmentation, do you just stay
on this one concentrated plane of consciousness
or do you move to other times and other places?
The human being remains in the usual
terrestrial fragmentation.

Does the Angel expand to many purposes at once?
Oh, yes, but that has nothing to do
with the purpose of human involvement.
You distribute *Yourselves* across
the entire span of creation.
Nothing is created in any realm
that does not hold *Your* consciousness,
is not a product of *You*.

From within your blindfolds of the present day,
you cannot know what these things might possibly be.
It is a comforting assurance to realize
that although you may fragment
into the many many selves that you need to become,
which may seem to be a staggering immensity
to the human mind,
that is merely a droplet in the ocean of what it is
in that same moment that you are accomplishing
in the name of creation.

Why is this so hard to understand?

Intellect insists that there is human,
physical, fillable space.
It is not comfortable with any other concept.
It advises, "You were and you will be,"
as though you traveled along a mapped road.
Another misconception.
Nothing stretches before you or behind you
but the void.

Will there be someplace to put your foot?
Not until you get there.
It is both a challenging concept and a freeing one.
So when we tell you that with the next inhalation
you create all things in the name of Love,
do you see how beautifully your entire universe
could be re-formed in that one instant?

One can conjecture and write poetry
about such a strange and distant love affair
with oneself, and at the same time, dear ones,
where creation exists (and it exists wherever
you are) the one rule applies.
Creation can be found only in the moment of Now.
I urge you not to demand of the intellect
that it be comfortable with anything I have just said.

Let your hearts sing
because the excitement of the truth
is that at any moment,
with just your loving presence,
all things can be joined.

What can you tell us about past lives?

Mind's curiosity is not Angels' curiosity.
A discussion of past lives certainly tosses a bone
to the curious mind of the human being,
but if it does not fulfill the purpose
for which we come together,
we cannot usefully expand on it too greatly.

The difficulty is that past lives
register with such reverberating importance
within the planetary consciousness,
yet beyond this arena they are of little import.

Are they real?

Yes and no.
Your human world is porous and so are you.
Your body is a receiver and giver of Light
as if you were a crystal barely covered
by tissues of the body.
It seems as though the consciousness
in this package moves through layers
of sequential understandings.
Since beyond the human illusion, time is not,
your lives, though they may seem to be past or future,
are accumulated in the presence of the you
of here and now.

Memory of past life is real.
There is the Oneness of which you are all a part,
but it does not hold minute individual detail.
We are speaking of many layers of awareness.
You, the Angel, never left Home,
yet you are here in physical form.
You are always and ever perfect Love,
and yet you walk in the world of darkness,
illusion, and separation and at times
you find it impossible to love anything at all.
Is that contradiction?
Beyond the cocoon of mind's domain, it is not.

Eternity has no time.
The intellect, when it hears the word "eternity,"
can race to here and beyond,
but the truth is that eternity doesn't go anywhere.
It just is. Quite as *You* just are.

Enjoy your past lives, things you have done,
things you hope to remember,
things that bring you pleasure.

Moments of real Love
(and there are always more in your lives
than you think) are the spark of the Angel.
Does Love get caught in illusion?
Yes, and it is immediately distorted.
But the spark is real.

When you leave the human world,
the only gift you bring Home is your Love.

**Did I know I was going to incarnate
in this body as *me?***

More or less, you did.
You are called by Love
to those who will give you birth.
This Love knows its way.
The Angel knows why it manifested
in a particular family, in a certain body,
and it knows what is to be accomplished
in a lifetime.
It does not know in minute detail how.
Within the realm of your humanness
you have free choice, but only to the degree
that it will ultimately honor the journey of the soul.

Human beings, in their understandable disquiet,
abhor surprises. Angels delight in them.
In fact, that is what they find inspiring
and compelling about the human journey.
It cannot be so stringently mapped because you create
the next moment of your life with every breath,
yet you cannot go beyond the boundaries
of the blueprint that the soul, in its infinite wisdom,
has masterminded.

So trust that however handy or unhandy
a physical body may appear to you,
the journey for which you have come
is being honored.
At the same time, you are perfectly free
to wander off on side excursions.
They will not cause you to miss your destination.

**Will knowing my past lives
help me know my purpose?**

Past lives hold a mystical fascination,
but do they serve the experiences
and the accumulations of this life?
Not really. They satisfy curiosity
and they give you hope,
for if you touch the memory of a past life,
you know you have lived before
and so it is reasonable that you will live again.
At times such memories explain the presence
of a deeply ingrained habit.

If you are to be free to live fully,
I would strongly suggest that you not only release
the power that you believe a past life holds,
but that you begin to sever relationship
most lovingly with your most recent past
in *this* life.

Freedom comes from self-love
and self-acceptance.
Where, in your experience *now*,
you find you are unwilling to grant yourself
these fundamental rights,
then certainly past history can shed light
on the root of the false belief
that bars you from your own heart.
Knowledge of past lives can be useful
only insofar as it illuminates this moment.

History seems to call you back in time
and you remain there.
You live your life now,
saying, "But I was an abused child." Yes.
Forty years ago perhaps you were.
That does not mean to minimize the suffering,
but neither does it call you to make a holy temple of it.
The soul is wise. It chose the labyrinthian pathways
that would bring you to this moment.
You would not be who you are now
if you had not lived what you lived then.

Does that mean that my suffering was all right back then?

It was all right for the soul's purpose
and it was not all right for the abused child,
and here you are.
Can you go back and avoid one blow, one lie,
one sexual attack, one moment of pain?
You can go back to understand
and bring that knowing to the you
of this moment who is still holding the defense
and bitterness of a childhood that was painful.
Honor the suffering by allowing that child
to become the compassionate adult of today.

Do we have lives of karmic completion?

When you speak of karmic completion,
you are of course referring
to the tying up of loose ends from past lives.

The mind feels more at ease
with the idea of karmic settlement than does the heart.
I say this so that you do not hold too tightly
to concepts like "karmic retribution,"
"karmic completion," or "karmic purpose."
Mind steadies itself with such ideas
in a world it fears is turmoil.

Let us alter the term "karmic completion"
to be understood as a life of fulfillment,
a life of awakening, a life of recognition
of things that need to be lovingly addressed,
but let us not say that you came burdened
from the womb.
The choice of family is Love, not karma.

The many things you believe must be done,
undone, atoned for, finished,
are just so much stuffing in the illusion
that distracts you from the Divine Light
of your own presence.
Your bookkeeping begins early,
I agree, but not before conception.

If you commit a crime in this life,
is there retribution in heaven?
When you step out of your bodies,
your deeds stand before you.
You see then what you have accomplished in your life.
Have you loved? Hated? Destroyed?
That is enough. Illusion is illusion.
It matters absolutely while you are engaged.
But when you leave, it matters not at all.

The moment of death is the moment of release,
of clarity, of absolute presence.
The learning is clear and intense,
but you also recognize that you are an Angel,
and what does an Angel have to learn?

You vow,
I will return again
and this time
I will not forget.

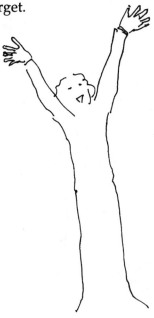

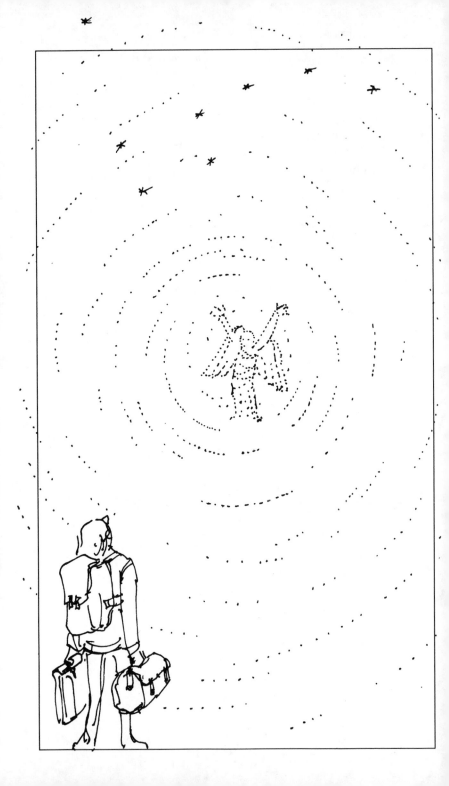

11
Multidimensional Travelers

*The center of creation can be likened
to a massive ball of infinite possibility.*

When you stand in the center of your human life,
you hold the profound position
of absolute authority.
There is nothing you do not know.
There is nothing unavailable to you.
With every breath you take you move
to the cutting edge of creation,
for nothing stretches out before you
save infinite possibility.
You are travelers without boundaries.

Mind insists that there is history.
You imagine your lives stretching behind you
and before you as though there were a path
already set down for you to walk upon.
There is no path.
The soul's wisdom knows its way.
In your exquisite wisdom *You*,
as Angel in the costume of this time,
expand All-That-Is into the void with each breath.
Facts are not facts at all.
You probably even think you are the same person
you were a few hours ago.

"Well," you say, "I look the same. I feel the same."

That is the costume.
Physically manifested reality clings to old form
more stubbornly than does the inner consciousness
which can create galaxies in a breath.
Who you were a moment ago is not who you are now,
because you have experienced more
and you have an expanded understanding.
If you would allow yourselves to live
with the concept that nothing
need remain permanently fixed,
you would save yourself a great deal of pain
and disappointment.
At the same time, you would give your dreams
freedom to move, your lives freedom to change,
and your wisdom freedom to speak.
One of the reasons that you are so unreceptive
to the truth of who *You* really are
is that you deny its ever-changing reality.

Let me describe for you the greater dimension
of which you are inevitably and eternally a part.
We are here to break the combination of the safe
wherein are kept the treasures
that go beyond knowing.

Spreading outward
from the edge of the consciousness of the Earth
there seems to be a canopy of stars.
Just to titillate your imagination a bit,
let me tell you that beyond the seeming
endless vault of your heavens,
there is another entirely different reality.
I speak of the fabric,
the texture of it, the design, the purpose.
One cannot begin to translate with precision
the nonphysical into physical terms
that would satisfy your habitual perspective.
But what of that?
Let us leave caution aside and plunge ahead.

If I were to grant you the magical wish
to be led beyond the human fold,
what do you suppose would be the call
that you would hear?

Schooled in the teachings,
you would reply, "Why, Love, of course."

Yes, indeed, but what would Love sound like?
Beyond physical ears, what is sound?
Beyond physical sight, what is vision?
Beyond physical emotion, what is Love?
These are questions that have seduced poet
and confounded philosopher
from the beginning of time.
So I begin not with apology,
but with the recognition that there is no hope for clarity,
only for the beginnings of wonder.

Hold a piece of dust in your hand
and give it absolute permission
to become its true nature.
You will find that you are holding Light,
crystals of consciousness that know everything
yet are unrecognized in the world.

If I were to describe a shimmering, brilliant,
dancing pathway beckoning to you
in the name of joy, it would come close,
yet it certainly would not be an exact description
of the nature of things.

How does one explain infinite opportunity
within the essence? The vibration of eternal hope?
The vision of perfect and ever-compassionate Love?

Imagine the most brilliant light
that you have ever seen
and it is but minimum wattage
compared to what is ever present
around the periphery of human awareness.
Yet you look into space and you see blackness.
Your scientists nod sagely and explain, "Well,
there are no particles there to reflect the sun."
It seems empty, a vacuum, but of course it is not.
I do not accuse the scientific world of bumbling,
but only of limiting themselves by the faith
they place in their instruments
and by the reverence
they offer their deductive minds.

What is magic
but the label the human mind
has offered to the truths you have forgotten?

At the center
of all you see as physically manifested reality,
there is the one spark of eternal and
ever-brilliant Truth.
It dwells not only in the core of the Earth
and surrounding all the planets
that are visible and known,
but blazes within each cell, within each molecule
of the corporeal dimension.
Every thought holds that same eternal
and indescribable brilliance.

Step free of the illusion of limitation.
You are not bodies.
You are Ideas—
brilliant, shining, living *thoughts* of the Angel,
having become manifest only in the dusting,
for the essence remains always true
to its own nature.

What more does your heart need to know?

Let me offer you some "Angel" practice.

Start by sitting quietly for a few minutes
and observe the rhythm of your own breathing.

Imagine yourself standing at the edge of the void,
with infinite possibility awaiting you.
With every breath you take,
you virtually create yourself anew.
With your every exhalation, all that is in you dies.

The instant when you release the breath
is the most important moment of your life.
At your exhalation you can, if you are willing,
release yourself from history and fly unencumbered.
Then, as you breathe in, you are free once more
to create in the name of Love.

With each breath you take, the doors open.
Each breath is an opportunity to touch Oneness.
And so you enter into dialogue between Angel
and human.

At times you will feel that there is no reality
but the physical one.
Then, in a breath or two,
you will find waiting for you the vastness
that honors both human and Divine.
The God you thought of as distant
will take up residence in your heart.
The heaven that you were taught is far away
will rest at your fingertips.

Speak to me on reading clouds, crystals ,
and talking to trees.

Anything on your planet that opens your heart
speaks to you.
Anything that speaks to *you*, you speak to.

The world is filled with symbols.
Every symbol represents, in its essence,
the Love you thought you left behind
when you came to planet Earth.
One might almost say that these delightful things
you have mentioned
are simply pieces of *You*.

When you read clouds or when trees speak to you,
that is not so strange if you recognize
that every conversation
you have in your lifetime, held in truth,
is conversation with *Yourself*.

I do not say that to make you feel lonely—
to the contrary.
The *Self* I speak of is that vast *Self*
that you seek every minute as long as you
are walking upon the planet. It is that dear *Self*
you hope to see in the eyes of another,
the *Self* that whispers in the rustling trees
and sparkles in the crystal.
It is the *Self* that sings from the mountaintops
and echoes in the valley, glows in the rainbow,
sighs in the cadence of a spring rain,
and it is the *Self* that opens your own heart.
If these things were not who *You* really are,
would they bring you such joy?

What is at the core of the Earth, Emmanuel?
Is there a different form of consciousness there?

Absolutely.
What erupts as the molten flow
of the belching volcano carries
with it exquisite consciousness.

You might ask, "Do you mean to tell me
that lava rolling down the side of a mountain
is wisdom?"

Yes, I do.
It is wisdom in its passionate emergence
above the crust of the Earth.
You all come from such molten, vibrant aliveness,
but you have become rigid as you emerged
into the more tepid air
of intellect and social approval.

Can you view the newborn child
as the fluid core of the Earth,
having been touched by the miraculous,
shrieking journey from Oneness
into the fragmented human form?
One wonders what becomes of the molten center
of one's own humanness.
Why, it becomes less and less believed in,
less and less heated until it, too,
becomes for many just dense frozen matter.

The core of the Earth
is precisely what *You* are without rigid form.
It is, indeed, at a temperature of seething intensity,
and yet if you were to walk into that fiery essence,
your bodies would disappear but *You* would not.

What does a crystal represent?

A thought made manifest.
Crystallized remembering.
This is true not only of crystals,
which are so evident in their beauty
and their mystery that they are precious symbols,
but everything upon the planet and beyond
speaks to you as well.
The molten core of the Earth is frozen in a crystal.
That is not all.
The consciousness of the Angel,
the movement of the river,
the flight of a bird, the growth of the grass,
they, too, are contained in the crystal.
Why?
Because all things come
from the same unique Oneness,
the same Eternal Consciousness.

Things take different forms,
but they are not the form they take.
You all take different forms.
You are not the forms you take.

Sometimes in silence I think I hear words spoken.
Then my mind intrudes and the words are gone.
Any suggestions?

The messages that you wish to receive
are already there and you have heard correctly.
Since you dare not believe that,
I have an exercise for you.

Whenever you feel the longing to hear
beyond your physical ears, kneel, bend over,
and place your forehead on the floor. Just that.

Allow your heart to rise above
the demands of your head.
Learn to listen in that position.

From listening right side up,
you have become accustomed
to the crushing weight of your opinion.
Listen upside down and see the benefit it brings.

Do I advise this practice for everyone all the time?
I mean it for some, and for those
who take comfort in turning things topsy-turvy
from time to time to break the chain reactions
of a lifetime.

Are there any animal forms
that were almost created to live on planet Earth
but then were not?

Take one or two or three of your favorites,
blend them together,
stir them up in your imagination,
and see what comes out—an elephant
with the loving eyes of a doe,
a crocodile that sings like a bird?
You can take all the pieces of Love
and bring them together,
but you might also conclude, "No,
though this one creature may be formed
out of all the Love that I can imagine,
it cannot really serve in this way.
It would be a hopeless, entangled contradiction."

Love comes in Oneness and then must separate.
It becomes not the singing crocodile,
but a reptile and a bird.
In fragmentation it becomes more rather than less,
because then it can know the nature
of both birdhood and crocodiledom.

When you all come from Oneness,
you separate first into man or woman.
That seems a decisive separation,
though I assure you it is not.
You take different nationalities,
different shapes, capacities, talents,
different dreams, different hopes.

You look at each other and you say,
"I don't see Oneness here. All I see is difference."

Yet how else could perfect Love forge for Itself
an adventure that would honor every bit of Itself—
each small exploration, every wandering
down some unknown path—
if It did not let Itself become the many?
The journey moves then from many to few,
and from few back to One.

On the way, are there singing crocodiles?
There will be, but perhaps not
that human beings can hear,
for the ears of humanity are coarse
and hear only what they expect.
Ask the Angel, "What do you hear
within the stem of the leaf?"
It will tell you, "Music."
"And what do you hear beyond
the croaking of the frogs?" "A symphony."

Is that imagination?
Not at all. I offer you a delightful experiment.
Design your own animals. Take bits and pieces
of all that you love, spin them around,
and give them breath.
Do you think that you will manifest something
in your living room that will roar and weep,
dance and thud? Perhaps.
And if this be so, where would you keep it?
Would you give it to the zoo?

These may seem childish questions,
but this is what is done.
That is why humanity has become so predictable,
so tailored to fear's design.
Each one of you holds inexhaustible potential
for creating anything at all.
What would you have? Play with this a little.
You will begin to see
even in the most mundane of creatures
the glory of unlimited possibility:
a giant squirrel, perhaps, ever benign,
willing to stand upon a street corner, cracking nuts
for the hungry.
Who is to say that this is not possible?

I have always sought the eruption of eternal wisdom.
What do you recommend so that I can crack apart?

I would recommend that you see
with infinite kindness the incrustation.
That is the first and most important suggestion.
The incrustation is not the enemy
of the eternal vibrancy
that is pulsating within you,
but only the necessary camouflage for a time.

Touch tenderly all aspects of your humanness,
but do not perceive it as an effective limitation.
You will not need to crack it open.
Caress it with softness
and you allow it to become more amenable
to the need of the inner core.

Do not attempt to understand this core
of eternal wisdom you seek to release,
for in that very hope of understanding,
you dust it again with limitation.
Remind it, "I greet you. I celebrate you,
even though I do not know what you are,
where you are, or what it is I am supposed to be doing."
There is only one lens—your own.
Through that lens, no matter how restricted
or expanded it may be,
you perceive the life you experience.

I would present another viewpoint.
Take the essence of human birth,
give it a vastness incomprehensible,
a consciousness absolutely beyond understanding,
a power that exceeds anything that anyone
has ever touched, and then give it wings.

When I say you are Angel first
and human second,
I mean you are the center of the Earth
and then you stand upon it.

Self-identity has been so limited
that you truly have forgotten that you
and the vibrant pulsation of the Earth
are of the same substance.
So we move to the edge and we leap beyond,
knowing full well that there are lines of terror
that hold us, that we must be restrained
to the mind's acceptance
or there would be nothing to say at all.
There would be one directive in this book—*Leap.*

Emmanuel, should we jump
or do we allow ourselves to be jumped,
to strive or not to strive, to worry or just let things be?

What is that point on the head of a pin
where one can stand and yet be free to move
with every breeze
without losing that point of contact?
Most interesting and delicate.

Envision the leap?
Yes, but without demand.
Allow life to live you, knowing
you cannot hope to place it in some folder
of understanding.

Consider a river at its fullest, flowing unimpeded,
carrying with it what it must,
leaving behind what it will,
honoring its own course.
The river is not one solid mass of water,
but countless drops that dance and sing
and bump into rocks and bury themselves
in the silt and rise again to the top.
It is alive within itself and it is,
at the same time, totally inhabiting its flow.
Be like the river which says only yes.

Say yes to your no,
for if you are part of the river,
you are part of the journey.

**Emmanuel, are self-identity and Oneness the same thing?
Can they be in conflict?**

It depends on what you mean by "self."
If you speak of the greater *Self* in Oneness,
there is no difference.
If you speak of the self who wants to understand this,
then you move to separation
and a variance in identity.

Remember that eternity is alive.
It is not some whispered hope or anemic dream.
Eternity in a breath could create a thousand worlds
and people it with a million replicas
and nuances of what is here.
The essence of *You* and All-That-Is is One.

**If we understand a hologram,
can we understand ourselves better?
Is the universe a hologram?**

You live in a holographic universe,
but it is much vaster than that.
Where does the universe get its design?
What goes beyond what seems to be?
What is the essence of life itself,
all of it, the volcanic matter,
the breath of your bodies,
the rhythmic function of your internal organs,
the crystal, the river, consciousness exploding
to become every manifestation?
That is the holographic reference.
But what is consciousness? You must go beyond.

*The truth you long for cannot be sought.
In the act of seeking you deny it
because You are already what you seek.*

When I say fall in love with yourselves,
I do not refer to the tiny human personality only,
though that is a beginning.
I do not mean the human being in confusion
or even falling in love with your falling in love.
It is just the first step of the way out of the mist.

There is no end to consciousness
and therefore there can be no receptacle
within which it can be placed for understanding.
Nothing can hold endlessness.
Is that not a joy and at the same time
does it not perturb that part of you which believes
that your only safety is in understanding?
The mind comes to the edge of its capacity
and becomes terrified.
It demands, "Tell me something else, Emmanuel!
Give me one more suggestion.
I'll do it. Just tell me."

What could I say? "All right, mind,
dissolve yourself. Be willing not to exist?"
Can you do that? Of course not.
That is not the nature of mind
any more than it's the nature
of a physically manifested body
to rush to its own death.
These restrictions keep you closeted
where your soul wishes to be,
but they are not who *You* are.

Comfort poor mind. It trembles.

**Emmanuel, would you tell us about other forms
of consciousness we don't see?**

That is not a simple question
because other forms of consciousness
that you don't see require various other
capacities of perception. Try this:

*Take a blade of grass (which is so simple
that I use it often and so accepted
that no one questions the fact
that there is grass).
Sit with it and look at it.*

*Hold a sensitive and softened vision.
Maintain the vigil until the imagination is invited in.*

*You will begin to see form upon form upon form existing
both within the molecular structure
and beyond it.
If you hold your gaze soft and steady,
you will see the dance of eternity
at the tip of the blade.*

There is magic in everything
because there is truth in everything,
there is eternity in everything.

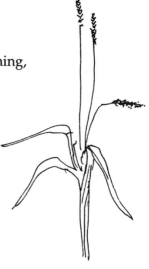

Are there forms existing beyond the perceivable?
Countless. They come and they go.
You create them and you dissipate them.

"And what of this?" you say,
and you create a spinning globe
that contains such mystery that the human mind
would be content to remain there for eons,
exploring.

You dance with your creations,
and toss another dream up into the heavens
to become a million stars that can never be seen,
not because they are not bright enough,
but because they are too brilliant
and the telescopes and vision of humanity
function only within a certain range of perception.

Why don't we see more?

Physical eyes,
by their necessary and deliberate design,
have only a specific range of capability.
With the sun's most brilliant light, you complain,
"It's so bright I can't look at it." Imagine.
The sun is a physically manifested creation
of an Idea that is hundreds, thousands,
millions of times brighter than the sun itself.
Of course the eyes cannot receive it.

There are colors beyond the palette
of human postulation.
Your physical eyes cannot admit them.
Will you ever behold those things? Yes.
You are part of the consciousness
that designed them,
but while you are locked in human packaging,
you can only imagine.

If you could expand your capacity
to see what dwells in the twilight,
what dances in the sunlight,
and what drifts in the night,
you would see that you are bumping
into Angels all the time.

Look at a rainbow
and you think you see wonderful hues,
magical and reflective,
the familiar prism of human color.
Do you believe that is all you see?
There is so much more.
Heavenly Beings rejoicing
upon every ribbon of Light,
forms coming into being and disintegrating,
breath by breath, instant by instant.
It is happening all around you.

Live your lives in expanded curiosity,
wondering "what if?" Censor nothing.
Mystery is mystery because it cannot be understood.
So follow the mystery.
It will bring clearing vision.

On finding your way:

The doors of life are mismarked.
The ones that say "EXIT" are really entrances.
And the ones marked "ENTRANCE"
are really exits.
There are doors that are labeled
"morning," "evening," afternoon,"
"childhood," "puberty," "maturity,"
"old age," "death."
Some say "education,"
others "understanding."
Some are marked "idiocy," others "breakdown."
They all seem to have a label
that would appear to indicate what to expect
when you open that door.
None of it is true.

You follow road signs
believing that you know where you are going.
In fact, you do not know and that is not insulting.
It is freeing. "Well," you say,
"I'm getting into my car in a little while and I *know*
where I'm going." Do you?
You may know the road you are following
but do you know where you are going?
Do you know who you are?
Do you really believe you have a destination
on planet Earth?
The only purpose for your existence is to *be*.

In moments of brilliance,
when you know you are nothing but Love,
mind declares, "I've come to my destination!"
No, you have not.
Love is not a destination.
It is a river.

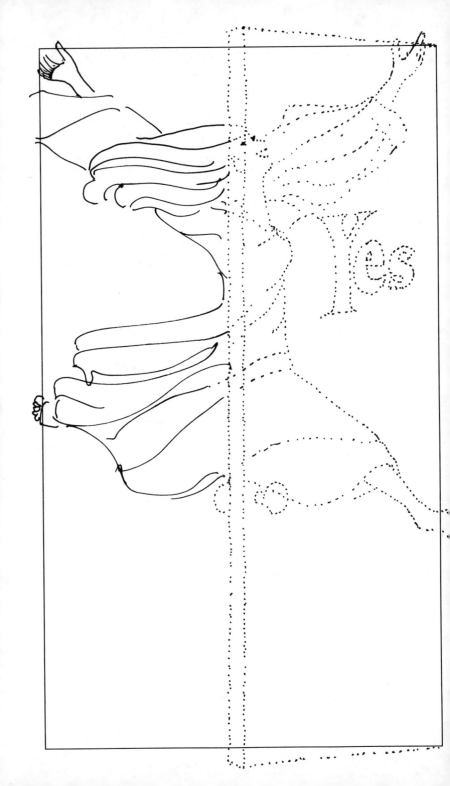

12
...and the Word
Was Yes

Spirit and human come together only
through the doorway marked Yes...

The Bible reads, "In the beginning was the Word..."
What was the Word?

The Word was *yes*.
When one is creating, the word is always *yes*.
When you, the human being, are present in the moment,
the Angel is there.
There is no more powerful *yes*
upon your planet than that.

Each one of you,
in your angelhood, has brought the *yes*.
No matter how troubled the human being may be,
nor how despicable he is considered,
there is always a moment of *yes* in that life.
Yes is the nature of the heart.

Each moment of *yes* that comes upon the planet
is that miracle of transformation
that brings the entire planet and all things upon it
that much closer to the time of Homecoming.

**If we are perfect to begin with,
why did we put ourselves through life's disturbing
experiences? Did we say yes to all that?**

The difficulty is that when one is locked in illusion,
one cannot imagine why
one would choose such a path.
When you are in Oneness, *You* see the world
of human endeavor as a blessed opportunity,
a most holy task that will allow you
to bring the loveliness, the grace,
the perfection of who *You* are
into the world of imperfection.

You look with Love
upon your planet from the Oneness,
and you declare, "I will go back. I will. I will.
I know I will forget and feel pain and fear,
but I will bring the truth of God within, the Angel.
I will walk the Earth again and again
until all those who are planetary Angels
transform the very nature of Earth experience
by the presence of their remembered Love."

In order to do this,
you yourself must wander for a time in the illusion,
believing every bit of it—almost.
It was in order to remember
that you went through life's disturbing experiences.
You have no idea of the miracle of the *yes*
that has brought you to this point of understanding.

You entered the darkness to believe in it
but not enough to extinguish the flame
of your Divine purpose.

Your yes *in the center of* no
is a leap of faith in the heart of doubt.

By your remembering,
the Light begins to emerge, the darkness dissipates,
and the wonder of who *You* are illuminates the world.
Yes replaces every *no* that you have ever uttered.
All is touched in this moment by the flame
that you have honored secretly, courageously,
and now consciously in your life.
If the Angel had not been willing to enter
into forgetting, the Angel could not bring the gift
that is born of that struggle.
You are about the business of transformation,
all of you.

**What happens when we say yes to love
with another human being who later leaves us?**

Once you have loved,
that bonding is there and will remain cohesive.
You will forever be at one.
I know for some of you
this does not seem desirable.
You are angry. You feel victimized
by the incapacity of another human being
to honor the love
that you believe you brought to him or her.

Times change.
People take different roads.
You shake your head sadly. "Well, that wasn't Love.
It didn't last forever."

Indeed, sometimes it lasts only for a week or so.
Every time you say *yes*, I want you to know
that what you are saying *yes* to is perfect Love.
It may seem that perfect Love
cannot last upon your planet,
but that is as much an illusion as anything else.

If you will put all disappointment aside
for a moment and just feel your heart,
you will see that the Love
that called you together is still there.
It does not mean that you have to live it together.
You need only remember it.
In the remembering, I promise you,
miracles will happen.
All the wounds, all the unfinished business,
will just fade away.

Why do I speak so often of humanness and Love?
Because that is the purpose of your journey,
the confusions of your life,
the wanderings of your mind,
and the sorrows of your heart.
You come in the name of perfect Love
and you spend your lives
attempting to honor that Love.
Along the way you find chagrin,
pain, regrets, lack of success.
You wonder, "What is it all about?"

Whatever your predicament may be,
yes will not solve it. It will dissolve it.
Yes is not obedience or acquiescence.
It is an embrace.

How can I say yes at times when all I feel is fear?

Whenever you feel fear, say *yes* to it
and move as quickly as you can
to be present in that moment.
Do not try to understand or argue with it.
Your acceptance is the catalyst to freedom.

What is it like when we remember?

When an Angel remembers within human form,
that Angel does not judge
or dismiss the human suffering
that has allowed that moment of Grace.
The Angel in you honors the human being.
It does not supplant it.

Be present in your suffering.
Do not try to avoid it.
When you are not present,
illusion is given the chance to build
enormous storm clouds of terror.
Say *yes* to whatever is there before you.
See what happens to terror
when you jump into the middle of it.
Find out what happens to pain when you accept it.

You are Angels of eternal mercy,
absolute Love, and everlasting presence.
You are one hundred percent human
at the same time
that you are one hundred percent Divine.
The blending of the two is the joy of your journey
and the blessedness of your gift.
You come into your world
ultimately to accept every piece of it.
The only doorway through which the Angel can enter
is through the doorway of *yes*.

There is a greatness in each one of you.
As you let that greatness emerge,
it graces the world.
Do not resist transformation
in the name of your old loyalty to pain.

When you have full memory of your own Divinity,
everything in your life becomes a blessing.
The suffering is seen for what it really is—
the next twirl in the dance.

The Angel resists nothing.

What is my next step?

Your soul is going to do what it must.
There is nothing that you can devise
to minimize, to distract, or to divert
you from your path.

As you go forward, step by step, inch by inch,
struggle by struggle, or resistance by resistance,
however you choose to move
in the direction of your call,
you will find that once you say *yes*
to any given moment, it will all become
very familiar to you.

You are looking for the next step?
Let your soul guide you.
You will move with whatever golden intent
rests within you to fulfill Love's call
as it reaches you.
In whatever vocabulary it comes,
you will know it and follow.

There is no one way
to live your life.
There is only the step-by-step adventure
with no knowable distant plan.
When one is saying yes,
it does not matter
upon what the foot rests
at a step's completion.
Wherever it is,
it will be the perfect place
to say yes *again.*

Here is a practice
to help you familiarize yourselves
with the gifts of this flowing
and transcendent word.

Sit in your inner silence for a time
and breathe the word yes
in and out of your heart.
Allow the mind to soften its hold.

As you allow yourselves
to experience physically breathing
into the next moment of yes,
you will find your chest filling,
softening all the no's
you ever learned to say.

Let the knowings of comfort,
of truth, of Love come to you,
and receive them as your own.

Let yes *become your mantra,*
your magical key,
your silent friend.

Can I will myself to say yes?

You can will yourself to say anything,
but you cannot will yourself
to believe in it.
The first time you said *no*,
you didn't believe it either,
nor the second,
nor the third.
It was just behavior.
With repetition, it becomes a habit and, finally,
it comes to be a point of self-identification.
So go ahead and will yourself to say *yes*.

Mind will tell you, " But I don't believe it."

Reassure mind, "It's all right, just say it again."

Mind will balk. "What are you doing? I don't even
know what the word means here."

You peacefully answer, "Yes."

This depth of acceptance has to be a conscious,
sometimes forced decision in the beginning.
You are going against the habits of a lifetime.
You are not aware of those times
when you close your heart and say *no*
only because it is such a highly developed skill
at this point that it has become something
you do without thinking. *Yes* requires practice.
Faith requires practice.
The allowing of Love requires practice.
It is all a choice.

Let me tell you something encouraging.
For every *yes* you say,
there is much more
than one *no* that is canceled.
One might consider it
as though one day of *yeas*
cancels out three years of *nays*,
just as one moment of Love
can erase forever
all the hate one has held in one's heart.

In the beginning your *yes* requires will.
It demands courage.
The *yes* may last as long as it takes you to say
that three-letter word and then it will vanish.
Say it again.
Find yourself a talisman to remind you.
Some of you have those unfortunate watches
that sound the hour.
Utilize even that. "Aha, the bell of awakening.
I will say *yes* now."

Mind wonders,
"How do I know what I am saying yes to?"

You don't,
and so begins
the adventure.

And so I bid you Godspeed.

This is your journey.
You have come
to sew up the tattered fabric
of human misconception,
to believe no longer
in the fragmented separation
of self from Self.

You are ready to bring
the you and the You together
to allow what it is that your soul,
in its profound and eternal wisdom,
has chosen.

Never disdain your humanness
but embrace it in the Angel wings
that are your own.

Twenty Years with Emmanuel

This business of living with the awareness of spirit is
both a joyful blessing and a challenge. Let me explain.

Those Grace-filled moments when I am actually channeling
Emmanuel are unspeakable in their wonder.
I am filled with the teachings and with the Love that the
teaching represents.

When the sessions, workshops, lectures come to an end,
I find myself just "me" again. My mind says I should be
changed, at least permanently uplifted. At the very
least not so easily drawn into "life" again, but that isn't
how it is.

Not only am I not removed and insulated from what is
happening, but it is my experience that the process of being
with Emmanuel has removed, bit by bit, the defenses that
fear promised would keep me safe. So I find myself more
and more open to everything.
Sometimes a butterfly can bring tears of joy or grief.
Sometimes I don't know the difference.

Some believe that if you walk consciously with spirit you don't have to hurt. I've found that isn't true for me. Without the accustomed barriers, life is free to blow through unimpeded. That's become the biggest learning and the greatest gift. Do I like being my human, sometimes frightened, and pained self? No. Is it all right? Thanks to Emmanuel's presence in my life, Yes.

So the dance of human/Angel goes on. I pray for the peace of enlightenment for all of us. And whenever I can remember, I celebrate whatever is. My gratitude to Emmanuel is truly eternal.

Pat Rodegast

In Acknowledgment:

I want to take a brief moment to present to
the world a thumbnail sketch of the Angels
who have been most deeply involved in the
production of this work. Both are women
of some age and experience. Both have
drunk deeply from the well of life. Both have
maintained their vigilance in the
midst of confusion and have developed a
most delightful as well as essential sense
of humor surrounding themselves and
whatever it is that comes their way.

In a word, they are very "normal," a
necessary quality for this enterprise. For
in such work, there is no room for ego,
personal ambition, unbecoming
somberness, or over-identification with
such words as "holy" or "astonishing" in
the self-serving aspect with which these
labels can be used.

The door to Love is open to all. What is
required is profound longing and
willingness to honor that call with
dedication. This, these dear ladies have
done with charm and grace and we in spirit
are most grateful. The work could not be
done without them.

Emmanuel